The Illustrated Guide to Worcester Porcelain
1751–1793

Other books by Henry Sandon:

ROYAL WORCESTER PORCELAIN
from 1862 to the present day

Superb hexagonal vase and cover, painted with underglaze scale blue ground reserving panels in which are painted fabulous birds and insects in onglaze enamels. Height 16½ inches; mark: a fretted square in underglaze blue. Worcester, Dr. Wall Period, c. 1775.

The Illustrated Guide to

WORCESTER PORCELAIN
1751–1793

HENRY SANDON

Curator of the Dyson Perrins Museum
and the Worcester Royal Porcelain
Company Limited

THIRD EDITION

BARRIE & JENKINS

London Melbourne Sydney Auckland Johannesburg

Barrie & Jenkins Ltd

An imprint of the Hutchinson Publishing Group

3 Fitzroy Square, London W1P 6JD

Hutchinson Group (Australia) Pty Ltd
30-32 Cremorne Street, Richmond South, Victoria 3121
PO Box 151, Broadway, New South Wales 2007

Hutchinson Group (NZ) Ltd
32-34 View Road, PO Box 40-086, Glenfield, Auckland 10

Hutchinson Group (SA) (Pty) Ltd
PO Box 337, Bergvlei 2012, South Africa

First published 1969 by Herbert Jenkins Limited
Second edition 1974
Third edition 1980

© Henry Sandon, 1969, 1974, 1980

Printed and bound in Great Britain by
Butler & Tanner Ltd, Frome and London

ISBN 0 09 142110 1

Contents

List of Plates

General Preface

This book and *The Illustrated Guide to Lowestoft Porcelain* constitutes the first two volumes in a series which has been designed to give new factual information to the collecting public in a straightforward helpful manner. The authoritative text is, in all cases, supported by a new range of illustrations showing in a clear manner typical and key shapes or designs. These *Illustrated Guides* will prove of great interest to the established and advanced collector as well as to the beginner, who will be given a firm foundation to a lifetime's pleasure.

For this book, the publishers have been most fortunate in enlisting the services of such a knowledgeable expert as Mr. Henry Sandon, the Curator of the Worcester Works Museum. Recently, Mr. Sandon, helped by a small band of enthusiasts, has excavated part of the site of the original Worcester factory, uncovering—after some two hundred years—thousands of discarded factory 'wasters'. Examination of these 'key' pieces has allowed the author to tell for the first time the true facts about eighteenth-century Worcester porcelain—facts which, in many cases, contradict the old cherished traditions. He has also given the collector new shapes to seek out and has thrown fresh light on the little understood Davis/Flight period (1776–93)—many products of which have only been identified since 1967, having previously been classed as of Caughley origin.

This book, with *The Illustrated Guide to Lowestoft Porcelain*, sets a high standard which the editor and publishers aim to maintain in other works by expert authors. Future titles are Rockingham Porcelain; Mason's Ironstone Ware; Liverpool Porcelain; Staffordshire Salt-glazed Stoneware; Ridgway Porcelain; Daniel Porcelain; and other works will be added to enlarge the scope of what I hope will prove a helpful and instructive series.

GEOFFREY A. GODDEN
General Editor

Author's Preface to the First Edition

Of the making of books about Worcester Porcelain of the First or Dr. Wall Period, there seems to be no end.

I suppose that more words have been written about the products of this factory and period (1751–83) than about all the other English porcelain factories put together—which is not surprising in view of the consistently high standard of the ware and the fact that Worcester is the only one of those many factories founded in the mid-eighteenth century to have continued an unbroken tradition to this day. This book, however, marks a milestone in the knowledge and appreciation of the products of this early period in that it is the result of discoveries made during an extensive archaeological excavation of the original site directed by the author. All previous books have ascribed shapes and patterns to Worcester merely by aesthetic reasoning; this is the first opportunity to relate them to ware which can be proved to originate from this factory.

The marking of English factory-produced pieces in the eighteenth century was very haphazard. In the case of Worcester, it is probable that it was some years after the founding of the factory in 1751 that the early factory-marks of the crescent and the 'W' began to be used, taking the place of the earlier decorators' marks and symbols. To these were later added the square marks and the various copies of Chinese and European marks, although a large number of pieces had no factory mark of any sort. This leaves a very great number of early ware of the Bristol/Worcester period which are unmarked, as also are very many pieces made after markings became more general. So one gets the position where a great collection such as that in the Dyson Perrins Museum has nearly as many unmarked pieces ascribed to Worcester's First Period as marked ones.

There is also the very large number of ware made in imitation of Worcester at such places as Caughley, Lowestoft and Liverpool. It is difficult for the ordinary collector to know from which factory these come, especially when some of them have confusing crescent marks. It must be a very brave, or foolhardy, person who can put his hand on his heart and say that he is always able to be positive about them from aesthetic reasoning alone.

What are the aesthetic reasonings that up to now have always decided whether a piece is Worcester or not?

The basis of them all must be the positive proved pieces, such as the 'Bristol' marked sauce-boats (the moulds of which were probably moved to Worcester after the Bristol factory was bought up); the sauce-boat marked 'Wigornia' (the Latinised name of Worcester); the two Corporation of Worcester jugs; the Worcester Parliamentary Election pieces; the 'King of Prussia' prints marked 'Worcester', and those with the heraldic arms of local families.

From an examination of these—their material, method of manufacture and form—a comparison with others that resemble them has led to a very wide body of pieces that have been *assumed* to be Worcester.

Now, for the first time, as a result of the excavation, it has been possible to prove positively a vast number of shapes and patterns to be Worcester; and from the finding of fragments in the form of wasters in different levels on the site, it is possible to build up a sequence of dating the development of the ware.

The finding on a kiln site of wasters in the biscuit (unglazed) state indicates almost beyond doubt that those pieces were made at that particular factory. Although it is possible to transport ware in the biscuit, it is not credible that eighteenth-century factories should send biscuit ware to each other for subsequent decoration, glazing and re-firing. Glazed ware, yes; for there is positive documentary evidence that this was done, as in the case of Worcester ware being sent to London for onglaze decoration in the 1760s and ware being bought by Chamberlain of Worcester from Turner at Caughley and from Flight at Worcester for gilding in the 1780s.

The finding of glazed fragments on a factory site is not proof that those particular vessels were made there, unless such glazed pieces are themselves wasters. In fact, a quantity of very strange 'foreigners' was found during the excavation, such as Chinese porcelain, delft ware from Lambeth and Bristol, Nottingham stoneware and Staffordshire saltglaze; but I am not suggesting that these were made by Worcester. The earthenware were probably odd vessels in use in the factory, and the Chinese ware were used either for study-ing, for copying of the patterns, or for crushing up and using in the body (an early recipe directs the use of 'foreign china'). One interesting fragment of Chinese blue and white was found which had been re-used by the factory as a colour trial.

The illustrations in the last section of this book show a great number of complete objects, from the Dyson Perrins Museum, of the period 1751–83, the earlier Bristol period and the subsequent early years of the Flight business, together with exactly matching fragments from the factory site—as far as possible in the biscuit—to prove these vessels as having been made at Worcester.

The usually sacred years of the First Period (often called the Dr. Wall

Period, although Dr. Wall died in 1776) have obviously to be reconsidered in the light of the excavation. So many Bristol-type shapes were found together with ware of the 1750s, and great quantities of ware of the Flight type in levels containing First Period ware, that it is clear that these periods overlap to a great extent; and in Chapter I, I suggest a new division of periods.

What can now be positively stated is that all the pieces shown in the photographs are of Worcester manufacture; and although a number of the shapes, patterns and factory marks shown are going to cause eyebrows to be raised, there can be no doubt whatever about their ascription.

Such proof has long been needed, as for many years it has been felt that a large number of shapes and patterns have been ascribed to the wrong factories and that a number of the oft-quoted easy methods of distinguishing Worcester—by such means as shape, pattern and translucency—are not consistent enough to be correct.

Awkward patterns which now have to change their allegiance include a number of printed scenes such as the 'Fisherman', which has always been called a Caughley pattern—*the positive Caughley pattern*—but which exists in a much finer printed Worcester version. Patterns are not the only things to have been found wanting in the cold light of archaeological investigation. For instance, the finding of disguised numeral marks, ware with orange or straw-coloured translucency and bases with undercut footrings—all features not previously associated with Worcester in most experts' minds—were finds that few people expected.

Some guidance on the ways of recognising Worcester ware is given in Chapter V, but it should be clear from the foregoing that the discoveries on the Warmstry House site cause a complete re-thinking in the methods of ascription of ware and that it is vital to rely on proved shapes from the site.

It should, however, be firmly stated that the excavation has shown how sound was the judgment in the past by so many great experts, in that very many of the shapes and patterns that have always been ascribed to Worcester were in fact found and proved. Here, especial praise must be given to R. W. Binns, Managing Director of the Worcester Royal Porcelain Company throughout most of the Victorian period. Working without many of the scientific and other advantages of the present time, it is a great tribute to his scholarship and practical understanding that so much of his pioneer work has been found to be accurate.

I realise that a great number of highly controversial facts will be revealed and a number of firmly established and long-held beliefs will be shaken; but the illustrations of the many unusual and unexpected pieces found on the site will ensure that a new look is taken at an old subject. They will cause many people to think afresh about the products of a great factory and help those who are new collectors to start off on the right foot.

Unless noted to the contrary, all pieces illustrated are in the Dyson Perrins Museum; and where no factory mark is given, it should be assumed that the piece does not have one.

Preface to the Third Edition

The printing of a third edition of this book has provided the opportunity to make some minor corrections in dating of the pieces illustrated and other adjustments following a number of archaeological excavations on Warmstry House in the summers of 1977, 78 and 79. These excavations have been important in confirming the results of the first dig, in tying up a number of loose ends and in extending our knowledge of the wares produced and the processes involved.

Acknowledgments

I would like to thank the many people who have assisted in the excavation, including members of the Worcester Archaeological Research Group and the Worcester Royal Porcelain Company—especially the members of the girl painters' department and David Peplow—and the many who travelled considerable distances to help, such as Mr. & Mrs. Roberts and family of Wellington, and Mr. and Mrs. F. A. Barrett; those who have given considerable help in the consideration of the material found—in particular Geoffrey Godden, Cyril Shingler and Dr. Bernard Watney; the Town Clerk and Corporation of the City of Worcester for their great kindness in allowing me to excavate on land belonging to them and to publish the resulting material and for permission to illustrate the map of the factory (Plate 149); the Directors of the Worcester Royal Porcelain Company—in particular Professor Baker—for their great encouragement in the whole project, and the Trustees of the Dyson Perrins Museum for their help and encouragement at all stages and in particular for kindly allowing me to use items in the Museum Collection to illustrate the book; Mr. T. G. Burn for allowing me to photograph a cup and saucer (Plate 106) from his Collection; Mr. G. A. Godden for allowing me to photograph some pieces in his Collection; Philip Barker, who gave great assistance in the consideration of the archaeological problems; and John Beckerley, who took all the photographs, which are such an important feature of this Illustrated Guide. Finally, especial thanks are due to Peter Ewence and Neal French, who are not only responsible for all the line drawings in this book but have given unstintingly of their time and knowledge at all stages of the work.

Chapter I

Warmstry House—Its History

The history of the Worcester Porcelain Company being so closely bound up with the premises in which the manufactory was established in 1751, it is only right to present an account of Warmstry House from contemporary documents, and of the excavation just completed, the results of which are given in the next chapter.

The first occupants of the site, an imposing position on a natural hill of sand and gravel which rises from the present river bridge to the far side of the Cathedral and the grounds of the present factory, were the Romans. The great defensive ditch of the Romano-British 3rd/4th century town, probably called Vertis, runs across the upper part of the site, guarding a crossing point of the River Severn, known as Sabrina by the Romans.

This river crossing explains the existence of the city of Worcester, and occupation sites going back as far as the early Iron Age have been found on this high ground.

Quantities of Roman and medieval pottery have been found on the site, mainly on the higher ground, a lot of it of local manufacture; and the existence of churches of both Saxon and Norman foundation near by show the continuous occupation that the area has enjoyed.

Warmstry House, a building of probable Tudor foundation, was originally the property of the Windsor family and the Earl of Plymouth. As late as 1837, the *Gentleman's Magazine* gives details of a curious armorial design carved in wood over the fireplace, which was the arms of Sir William, second Lord Windsor. The same article gives details of carvings from the building showing the arms of the Warmstry family, the successors to the Windsors, who produced several Registrars of the Cathedral and one who was the Dean of Worcester.

These arms are described as a cross molyn between four crescents, Warmstry quartering three lozenges in fesse, and Warmstry impaling a chevron between three mullets. The first part of the arms, involving the display of crescents, is interesting as being a probable explanation of the use of a crescent as one of the chief marks of the Worcester Porcelain Company – one

I

which forms part of the Company's trade mark to this day. A drawing of the arms (Fig. 1) above a memorial tablet to one of the Warmstry family in Worcester Cathedral may be of interest at this point.

The property passed into the hands of the Plowdens and then to the Reverend Chewning Blackmore, minister to the body of Independents from 1698 to 1737, who obviously used part of it for public worship up to the time it was sold to William Evett, a glover, in 1707 for an amount of £340. The indenture describes the property as 'that large house now or sometimes heretofore divided and used as several tenements and commonly called Warmstry House, part thereof being now used for the worship and service of God (by the Independents under Thomas Badland), with the gardens, orchard and

FIG. 1. Arms above memorial tablet in Worcester Cathedral.

bankside thereunto belonging, all which said premises are situated in a street called Saint Mary's Street, sometimes called Cowell Street and now commonly called by the name of Great Fish Street, and now or late in the possession of the several tenants, Samuel Clements, William Harris, Samuel Hill and Benjamin Cooke, Thomas Osborne living in a messuage on the south side of the way leading to Severn, formerly called Cowell's Load, now called Warmstry Slip'.

The Perrins Museum possesses an interesting oil painting on canvas showing the main riverside area of the city, including Warmstry House with its gardens stretching down the hill to the river wall. The painting depicts the gardens as having attractive ornamental shrubs and large sandstone walls, and must have been made before 1751 since it shows no signs of any factory buildings.

On May 16th, 1751, a lease of Warmstry House was granted by William Evett to Richard Holdship—who, like Evett, was a glover of the City of Worcester—for a term of twenty-one years at a yearly rent of £30, renewable at the end of that term for a further twenty-one years on payment of a fine of £20.

Thus was prepared the way, in the very next month—on June 4th, 1751—for the drawing up of the famous agreement founding the porcelain manufactory, described as 'Articles for carrying on the Worcester Tonquin Manufacture, June 1751'. The Worcester Royal Porcelain Company Limited, the successors of the original Company, still possess this fascinating document, which can be seen at their London showrooms. The twenty-nine articles that form the basis of the agreement have been published* and it will suffice for the purpose of this book to give the most important details and the names, occupations and the amounts of money that each of the original partners subscribed.

Articles

Whereas a new Manufacture of Earthen Ware has been invented by JOHN WALL of the City of Worcester Doctor of Physic and WILLIAM DAVIS of the same Apothecary under the denomination of Worcester Porcelain:

Now know all Men by these presents that in order to carry on the Manufacture the following persons and together with them the said JOHN WALL and WILLIAM DAVIS do agree to become subscribers and do hereby actually become subscribers for the following sums of money (that is to say)

WILLIAM BAYLIES of Evesham in the County of Worcester Doctor of Physic	£675
EDWARD CAVE of St. Johns Gate London Printer	£562. 10. 0.
RICHARD HOLDSHIP of the City of Worcester Glover	£562. 10. 0.
RICHARD BRODRIBB of Bevere in the County of Worcester Esquire	£225
JOHN BRODRIBB ⎱ of the City of Worcester, Woolen Drapers, as JOHN BERWICK ⎰ Copartners	£225
JOSIAH HOLDSHIP of the same Maltster	£450
JOHN THORNELOE of the same Gent.	£337. 10. 0.
DOCTOR JOHN WALL	£225
WILLIAM DAVIS	£225
EDWARD JACKSON of the City of Worcester Merchant	£225
SAMUEL BRADLEY of the same Goldsmith	£225
JOHN DOHARTY of Worcester Gent.	£225
SAMUEL PRITCHETT of Knightwick in the County of Worcester Clerk	£225
WILLIAM OLIVER of the City of Worcester Gent.	£112. 10. 0.

for raising a joint Capital Stock of Four thousand and five hundred pounds to be invested and employed in and relative to the carrying on of the said Manufacture of Porcelain in the said City of Worcester . . .

FIRST. That the said Manufacture shall be carryed on at the said City of Worcester in a certain House with the Buildings Gardens and appurtenances thereunto belonging situate in the Parish of Saint Alban in the said City for the term of Twenty one Years commencing from the twelfth day of July next for which term a Lease hath been taken by the said Richard Holdship of the said house and premises for that purpose for and on behalf of himself and the said other subscribers and inventors and that after the expiration of the said term if the said Manufacture shall be found to answer the same shall be continued and carryed on either there or in some other convenient place for so long time as the majority of the subscribers in value shall think fitt under and upon the same terms provisoes conditions covenants and agreements.

SECONDLY. That the said John Wall and William Davis do and shall discover as they hereby ingage and bind themselves to discover for the benefitt of themselves and the other subscribers the real true and full art mistery and secret by them hitherto invented and found out with such further improvements and secrets as shall from

---

* *Worcester Porcelain and Lund's Bristol*, Barrett, published by Faber & Faber.

time to time hereafter be made and found out by them or either of them for the making finishing or perfecting of the said ware and that they or either of them shall not directly or indirectly discover the art or secret which they now have or hereafter may acquire for the making or improving of the said ware unto any other person or persons whatsoever under the penalty of Four thousand pounds each to be forfeited divided and paid by the said John Wall and William Davis their respective Executors or Administrators unto the Treasurer of the said subscribers for the time being for the use of the said other subscribers their Executors or Administrators rateably and proportionably to the several sums for which they are respectively adventurers in this present Subscription but that the full and whole art mistery and secret discovered and to be discovered by the said John Wall and William Davis for the making finishing and perfecting of the said ware shall for ever hereafter remain the property of the said John Wall, William Davis and the said other subscribers rateably and in proportion to the sums for which they are severally subscribers and the said John Wall and William Davis shall each of them take and make a voluntarily Oath if required by the majority in value of the said other subscribers at a monthly meeting before a magistrate of the truth and reality of the discovery they have already made and of each particular further discovery and improvement they shall from time to time make of and in the art and mistery of making the said ware and the full and whole art and secret thereof so far as the said John Wall and William Davis are now masters of the same with the intire process thereof shall be fairly wrote out and subscribed with the proper hands and names of them the said John Wall and William Davis respectively and deposited locked up and secured in a box with three different locks and keys one of which keys shall be in the hands of the inventors and the other two in the hands of such persons as a majority in value of the other subscribers shall from time to time appoint and as to any new discoveries or improvements to be hereafter made by the said John Wall and William Davis or either of them in respect of the making or perfecting of the said ware the same shall as soon as the invention thereof shall be sufficiently established by experience in like manner be wrote out subscribed and secured in the said Box which shall be kept by the Treasurer for the time being.

THIRDLY. That the inventors the said John Wall and William Davis shall be paid Five hundred pounds to witt Two hundred and fifty pounds each out of the said Four thousand and five hundred pounds subscribed as aforesaid as a reward for such their discovery of the secret of making the said Porcelain which said Five hundred pounds they shall be allowed and obliged to subscribe into the capitall stock for carrying on of the said Manufacture and the same shall be the first money employed therein and the said John Wall and William Davis shall have a right to vote as subscribers in value for or in respect of the said Two hundred and Fifty pounds each as well as their other shares subscribed towards the said Capitall Stock.

FOURTHLY. That the said Capitall Stock of Four thousand and five hundred pounds shall be divided into forty five shares of One hundred pounds each of which five shall remain the property of the said John Wall and William Davis in respect of the said Five hundred pounds allowed to them as a reward for discovering the secret as aforesaid and the remaining forty shares shall remain the property of the said John Wall and William Davis and the said other subscribers in proportion to the several sums they subscribe towards making up the said Capital as aforesaid.

FIFTHLY. That as soon as ten pounds per centum per annum shall be raised from the neat and clear profitts of the said manufacture the said John Wall and William Davis shall be entitled to receive out of the said neat profitts the sum of One hundred pounds more as a further recompence for the discovery of the said Secret.

. . .

EIGHTEENTHLY. That all the materialls and utensills that the inventors are now possessed of and which are proper to carry on the work be purchased for the use of the subscribers at the just and real value thereof and as they shall be estimated by persons who are proper judges in that behalf and that the inventors be moreover impowered to purchase such materials as are necessary for commencing and carrying on the work and their account thereof admitted without producing such bills of parcels as may tend to discover the secrets of the said Manufacture so as the inventors by that means practice no fraud or imposition upon the other subscribers.

NINETEENTHLY. That the workmen and boys now employed by the inventors be deemed to have entered into the service of the subscribers in general in the said Manufacture from the eleventh day of May last.

TWENTIETHLY. That for the encouragement of Robert Podmore and John Lyes workmen who have for some time been employed by the inventors in the said Manufacture it is provided and agreed that over and above their usual wages the said Robert Podmore and John Lyes shall after ten pounds per cent per annum profitt shall be made of the said Manufacture be allowed such a gratuity out of the further profitts thereof as the majority in value of the subscribers shall determine not less than half one share of the profit of the said original stock the better to engage their fidelity to keep such part of the secret as may be intrusted to them and therefore it is further provided that in case the said Robert Podmore and John Lyes or either of them shall by any method way or means disclose any part of the secret Wherewith they shall be so intrusted or desert the service of the said subscribers that then the said Robert Podmore and John Lyes shall forfeit be liable and accountable to pay back unto the treasurer for the use of the said subscribers so much money as they shall have before received by such gratuity.

. . .

TWENTY-SECONDLY. That no strangers be admitted into the work but that every part thereof be conducted and carryed on with the greatest privacy secrecy and economy to which end it is provided that a clerk of the works shall be appointed who shall be also outward door keeper and keep the key thereof and that there shall be also an inner door with a different lock the key whereof shall be kept by the aforesaid Robert Podmore and John Lyes or whom else the committee shall appoint so that they and the clerks may be check upon each other.

. . .

The twenty-nine articles were signed and sealed by the fifteen subscribers on June 4th, 1751, Richard Brodribb having been appointed treasurer.

From the articles quoted, it would appear that the Company was formed for the express purpose of acquiring the secret formula and processes that had been invented by Dr. John Wall and William Davis, and that the two inventors had already been carrying out experiments. Two of the workmen, Podmore and Lyes, are specifically mentioned as having been employed on the experimental work and reference is made to the materials and utensils of which the inventors were in possession, and to workmen and boys who had been employed by them.

In return for this formula and for the work done on it and still to be done, Dr. Wall and Davis were to receive £250 each, which was to be regarded as their subscription; and after £10% clear profit had been made they were to receive a further £100 each. In that event, Podmore and Lyes were also each to be paid a gratuity.

Although the articles suggest that Dr. Wall and Davis invented the formula, it has long been felt that the formula and processes were those in use at the short-lived Bristol factory of Miller and Lund. A note in the *Bristol*

Intelligencer on July 24th, 1752, explains that the china manufactory in that city was 'now united with the Worcester Porcelain Company where for the future the whole business will be carried on'.*

An interesting reference to the Bristol factory appears in a letter from Dr. Richard Pococke—a great traveller and inveterate letter writer—to his mother. In this letter, dated November 2nd, 1750,† he refers to a visit, describing the manufactory as 'lately established here by one of the principal manufacturers at Limehouse which failed'. He goes on to describe the manufactory as 'Lowd'ns Glass House' and explains that 'they have two sorts of ware, one called Stone China which has a yellow cast, both in the ware and in the glazing, that I suppose is made of Pipe-clay and calcin'd Flint. The other they call Old China, this is whiter and I suppose this made of calcin'd flint and the Soapy rock at Lizard Point which 'tis known they use; this is painted blue ... they make very beautiful white sauce boats adorned with reliefs of festoons, which sell for sixteen shillings a pair.'

Little is known about the earlier Limehouse factory referred to 'that failed', no ware of this manufactory having ever been positively identified. An interesting account of the search for it is given in Dr. Bernard Watney's *English Blue and White Porcelain of the Eighteenth Century*, 1963.

Much more is known about the Bristol factory, which was to have such an important effect on the early years of the Worcester Porcelain Company. The establishing of the names of the owners of the Bristol factory—situated in a glasshouse in Redcliffe Backs—was done by Aubrey J. Toppin,‡ who was able to show from details in the bankruptcy proceedings of Richard Holdship that they were William Miller and Benjamin Lund.

The exact date when Miller, a grocer, and Lund, a brass founder, started manufacturing porcelain is unknown. A licence dated March 7th, 1748–49, was granted to Benjamin Lund to mine soapy rock at Gew Graze near the Lizard in Cornwall, and in November 1750 the factory was advertising for apprentices. Some of the products bear the embossed mark BRISTOL, sometimes spelt BRISTOLL (Plate 2) and one of these, the figure of the old Chinaman, is dated '1750'.

From these facts, it would not appear that the manufactory started much before the summer of 1749. The Richard Holdship bankruptcy proceedings referred to indicate that the Bristol factory was bought lock, stock and barrel by Holdship on behalf of the other Worcester partners on February 21st, 1752—that is, five months earlier than the *Bristol Intelligencer* described its local factory as having united with Worcester. It will therefore be clear that the Bristol factory lasted only some three years and at the end of this time the 'stock, utensils and effects and the process of manufacture' were moved to Worcester.

Included in this arrangement was the lease of the soapy rock mine and Richard Holdship's agreement to sell the material to his other partners at £18

---

* See Pountney, *Old Bristol Potteries*, pp. 192–204.

† British Museum Library, MSS Dept., Cat. No. 15800 (Private Letters).

‡ *English Ceramic Circle Transactions, Vol. 3, Part 3*, 1954.

a ton, to start from December 25th, 1751, with an agreed minimum of twenty tons per annum. The use of this soapy rock, or steatite, was the great key to the future success of Worcester, as porcelain made from it was able to withstand boiling liquid without cracking or crazing. Discoveries on the Warmstry House site show how well adapted was the recipe for the making and firing of the finest and most difficult objects.

It is obvious that the difficulties of differentiating between most of the Bristol and early Worcester ware are very great, made as they probably were out of the same moulds and material. A full discussion of this early ware is given in Chapter III. But before leaving Bristol finally for Worcester, one point arising out of Holdship's bankruptcy proceedings must be dealt with. In it the Bristol ware is described as 'in imitation of China Ware' and 'East India China Ware', whereas the Worcester factory made ware 'in imitation of Dresden Ware'. After the purchase of the Bristol factory, Worcester resolved to make ware of both China and Dresden.

What was the ware made in the first year at Worcester, between the setting up of the factory in June 1751, using the secret recipe of Dr. Wall and William Davis, and February 1752 when the Bristol recipe, and especially the use of the steatite or soap rock, was obtained? R. W. Binns* always affirmed that the earliest ware made at Worcester was of a frit paste body—that is, a soft paste porcelain composed mainly of a vitreous compound of silica and alkali, called a frit, which is fired, ground and mixed with white clay and lime. Although no such examples were found on the site, the difficulty of excavating the lowest levels because of the present water table does not allow certain proof that his theories were incorrect. Certain it is that no positive Worcester porcelain made from a frit body has yet been discovered.

On the other hand, there is no evidence that Worcester had been able to obtain steatite before December 25th, 1751. Until definite evidence of the products of the first year of Worcester comes to light, this period must remain a puzzle.

By August 1752, production at the new Worcester factory must have been far enough advanced for the *Gentleman's Magazine* (the editor of which was Edward Cave, one of the Worcester partners) to be able to publish an engraving showing the layout of the factory and to announce that 'A sale of this manufacture will begin at the Worcester Music Meeting, on September 20th, with great variety of ware, and 'tis said at a moderate price' (Plate 3).

Production of ware of all kinds was undertaken, from pieces painted in underglaze cobalt blue to coloured ware based on Chinese and Dresden styles—the emphasis being upon the useful rather than the ornamental. The only articles which seem to have given great difficulty were large plates.

One of the great advantages of the special 'secret' recipe was its ability to withstand hot liquid without cracking or crazing, faults to which the ware of most of the other English factories of the day was prone.

On June 18th, 1754, Edward Cave died and nine additional shareholders were brought in, making the number up to twenty-three. The new partners

* *A Century of Potting in the City of Worcester*, 1865.

were Reverend Benjamin Blayney; Robert Blayney; David Henry; his wife Mary; Reverend Richard Pritchett; William Russell, surgeon; Thomas Salway; John Stillingfleet; and Thomas Vernon, M.P.

In 1756, the following advertisement appeared in the *Public Advertiser* on March 4th:

> The Proprietors of the Worcester China Manufacture for the better accommodation of merchants and traders have opened a warehouse at London House, Aldergate Street, London, where they may be supplied every day, between the hours of nine in the morning and three in the afternoon, with assortment of goods wholesale on the most reasonable terms. Orders are likewise taken and executed with despatch for home and foreign trade.

A most interesting but undated price card for this warehouse is in the Dyson Perrins Museum at Worcester. As can be seen below, it gives some idea of the range of objects made and their wholesale prices—all quoted in dozens except for the tureens. The references to 1st, 2nd and 3rd are to the different sizes, 1st being the smallest.

				per dozen
Cups and Saucers, Quarter pint Basons & King's Coffees				3/6d.
Half pint Basons				6/-
Pint Basons and Quart Basons			9/-	15/-
Tea pots round 1st size				15/-
Tea pots 2nd & 3rd			21/-	27/-
Tea pots, Fluted pannel'd and Octagn.				30/-
Milk jugs round and press'd			8/-	12/-
Cream Ewers ribb'd and pannel'd				9/-
Coffee Cups and Cans				5/-
do. ribb'd and Wav'd				8/-
Decanters pint				21/-
do. Quart and 3 pint			30/-	42/-
Mugs Half Pint				10/-
do. Pint and Quart			10/-	24/-
Wash hand Basons				3/6
Chamber pots				4/-
Tureen round 1st and 2nd			each 7/6	12/6
do. oval 1st and 2nd			21/-	25/-
Tart pans 1st 2nd 3rd		4/-	6/-	8/-
Potting pans 1st 2nd 3rd		6/-	9/-	12/-
Two Handle Boats 1st 2nd 3rd		24/-	30/-	40/-
Pannel'd Boats 1st and 2nd			9/-	10/-
Fluted do. 1st and 2nd			12/-	15/-
Sauce-boats high footed 1st 2nd and 3rd		14/-	18/-	27/-
Partridges white 1st and 2nd			each 4/6	5/-
do. Enamel'd 1st and 2nd			each 7/-	8/-
Cornucopias 1st and 2nd			2/3	2/6
Potting pots and Covers white, Oval Basket work				2/6
Scallop'd Shells 1st 2nd 3rd and 4th	4/-	6/-	9/-	12/-
Vine Leaves 1st and 2nd			4/-	8/-

Fig Leaves	4/–	12/–
Dutch Jugs 1st and 2nd	3/6	8/–
Leaf Sauce-boats Enamel'd 1st and 2nd	3/–	3/6

'With many other various sorts, cheap in proportion:—
N.B. 15 Pr. Cent Discount will be allow'd for prompt payment.'

Most of these objects are gone into in greater detail in Chapter III, but it will be as well to explain that 'Partridges' are tureens in the form of a partridge sitting on its nest (Plate 114) and 'Dutch Jugs' are the jugs with mask spouts (Plate 42).

In the previous year, 1755, the first of several sales was held in London, when 300 lots were sold in a three-day sale at the Royal Exchange Coffee House.

The development of printing onglaze and, later, underglaze by Robert Hancock and Richard Holdship by 1755 and the production of splendid coloured grounds spread the fame of the Company.

At this time, the factory had as its focal point the great mansion itself—all of the rooms being used as workrooms, showrooms and offices, one being called the 'secret room' where, presumably, the secret formula was kept and experiments were done. The remainder of the buildings and the kilns were built in the gardens on the steeply sloping ground leading down to the river wall, most of these buildings running along Warmstry Slip. An excellent print of this period, engraved by Robert Hancock, shows the factory from the river—a river very different in appearance from that of today, now that the level has risen some eight feet since the locks were built downstream at Tewkesbury and just below Worcester. Before this time, the river was tidal and rather shallow, except for periodic flooding which has left its mark upon the site. Flat-bottom trows were a familiar sight, running up river from Bristol and making Worcester quite an important port. The print is reproduced in Plate 4 and trows can be seen, presumably having brought raw materials up river to the factory or loaded with finished ware for the journey back to Bristol.

The best description of the factory at this time is given in Valentine Green's delightful *Survey of the City of Worcester*, published in 1764. Green, famous as a historian of Worcester and Worcestershire, was employed by the Porcelain Company as an engraver under Robert Hancock, the man who had probably brought the process of printing on porcelain to the factory and who engraved most of the fine plates that appeared in the book.

Green explains that

Warmstry House was originally a large mansion-house which, with its adjacent offices, is converted to a pleasing scene of art and industry. Upon entrance of it, you are first conducted into the counting-house on the right-hand of the passage, and from thence into the throwing-room, where the ware is first formed from the clay. From this you are taken through a narrow passage, to the stove, which, a fire being placed on its centre, equally diffuses its heat to the whole; the ware is placed here to dry gradually, thereby preparing it for the succeeding operation. The next room shown is the great hall, where the ware is turned upon the lathe. In a little room adjoining, another method is carried on, called, pressing the ware on the wheel. In a great parlour of the opposite side of the building, is also turning on the lathe, with that part of the business called, handling and spouting, i.e. putting the hands to cups, etc. and the spouts to teapots, etc. From hence, you descend, by a flight of six or eight steps, into another pressing room, the action of which thus varies from the former; in this the clay is pressed by the hands only in the mould, but in the other by the means of a wheel. From hence you are conducted to the lower regions of this work, where are the first sett of kilns, called, buisket-kilns, in which the ware is first burnt. After passing another stove, you enter the dipping, or glazing room, in which the ware receives its glaze. From thence to another sett of kilns, where the glazed ware is burnt. Then, crossing the coal yard, you are shown a third sett, called streightening-kilns: in an adjoining room, the cases, or saggers, in which they burn the ware, are made. To the scraping room next shown, all the buisket ware is brought from the first mentioned sett of kilns, and there assorted. In the slip-house the different parts of the composition, being first levigated, are sifted thro' fine lawn seives, and promiscuously blended together, afterwards dried in the slip-kilns, which are similar to the pans used in making of salt. In a room adjoining to the slip-house, you are shown a large iron rowl, upwards of two tons weight, by the assistance of horses, revolving in a grove, (*sic*) not much unlike a cyder mill. This rowl reduces all the hard bodies made use of in the composition to a fine powder, fit for levigation. You at length enter the painting room, where the ware receives the ornamental part of the process, and which, after burning and assorting, is completed for sale. The curious and valuable art of transferring prints on porcelain is, in this factory, arrived at, and carried on in the greatest perfection. This work is the employ and subsistance of a great number of people.

On January 1st, 1763, a deed of lease was taken out on a grinding mill situated upon Glasshampton Brook in the Parish of Astley. The lease was for nine years, intended to expire at the same time as the lease on Warmstry House. In the same year, another plug for Worcester was given in the *Gentleman's Magazine*, in which Worcester ware was compared with imported porcelain:

> The Worcester has a good body, scarce inferior to that of Eastern china, it is equally tough and its glazing never cracks or scales off. But this is confined to few articles; the tea table, indeed, it completely furnishes; and some of it is so well enamelled as to resemble the finest foreign china so that it makes up costly sets that are broken without a perceptable difference.

A quantity of Worcester porcelain was sold in the white—that is, glazed but otherwise undecorated—by James Giles, the china decorator, of London. An advertisement in the *Public Advertiser* on January 28th, 1768, is headed 'J. Giles, China and Enamel Painter, Proprietor of the Worcester Porcelain Warehouse up one pair of stairs in Cockspur Street' and mentions a large stock of white goods available for enamelling, and that he could supply china painted 'to any patterns his patrons might chuse'.

A discussion on the decorations of the Giles artists can be found in Chapter III; but it may be noted here that the engagement in 1768 of painters from the Chelsea factory brought the great London experts in the painting of European styles to the Worcester factory, which had previously specialised in Oriental-stylework, although some European-style decoration had been done before this.

In 1769 Robert Hancock, the engraver, purchased the house next door to the factory referred to in the print seen in Plate 4 as Mr. Holdship's new buildings. Richard Holdship, one of the Holdship brothers, who it seems was closely involved in printing at Worcester, had earlier left the Company and gone to Duesbury's factory at Derby, where he passed on the secrets of making soapstone porcelain and printing and also agreed to supply soaprock. He had become a bankrupt in 1761, as previously mentioned, and sold his shares in the Worcester Porcelain Company to David Henry of London for a nominal sum of five shillings.

The main twenty-one-year lease of Warmstry House was drawing to a close, and in the *Worcester Journal* on December 5th, 1771, a sale of the Manufactory was announced as follows:

To be Sold by Public Auction, in one lot, to the best bidder, on Thursday, the Second day of January, 1772, at Eleven o'clock in the Forenoon, at the house of James Fewtrell, being the Hop Pole Inn, in the City of Worcester.

The genuine process of making Worcester Porcelain together with the stock, estate and effects of the Worcester Porcelain Company, comprehending the stock of materials, moulds, tools, utensils and kilns etc., employed in the said Manufactory house at Worcester, and the stock of ware, finished and unfinished, lying in the warehouses and rooms of the said manufactory house and marked and numbered according to inventories, which are to be prepared in due time before the day of sale. Also the leases of the said Manufactory house in Worcester and of the mills at Astley, in the County of Worcester, now occupied by the Company and of the adjoining farm; also sundry other messuages or tenements, freehold and leasehold situate near the said manufactory house, and the Company's interest in a mine of clay in Cornwall.

Further particulars may be known by applying to the principal clerk at the Manufactory house in Worcester aforesaid, or to the agent at the Company's warehouse No. 12 in Gough Square, Fleet Street, London.

N.B. The stock of ware and goods in the said warehouse in London will be sold separately in London, some time after the above sale in Worcester, of which due notice will be given; in the meantime, the trade will be carried on there without interruption, and all orders duly attended to and supplied.

The entire property of the Company was sold on January 2nd, 1772, for the sum of £5,250, the names of the fifteen vendors being given. The purchaser was announced to be the Reverend Thomas Vernon, one of the partners; but he gave up possession in favour of John Wall, Junior. This was just a temporary move pending the formation of a new Company on March 3rd, 1772. John Wall disposed of the property for a nominal sum of five shillings to his father and also to William Davis, apothecary; William Davis, gentleman; the Reverend Thomas Vernon; Robert Hancock, engraver; and Richard Cook of London.

So we see Robert Hancock firmly established as a partner in the new Company. But two years later, on October 31st, 1774, 'whereas certain controversies, differences and disputes had arisen between the partners touching the said Robert Hancock's share of the said stock, it was agreed by indenture in order to prevent all such disputes, to purchase from him his share in said stock for the sum of £900, being exactly one sixth'.

Hancock left for pastures new at the Caughley factory—forty miles or so up the River Severn, near Broseley—to join his one-time pupil Thomas Turner, probably taking with him a number of his copper plates. More is said later about the confusion that has arisen over the respective work of Worcester and Caughley from this period onwards, but it should be made clear that neither Turner nor Hancock can be accused of using the actual Worcester copper plates on their productions at Caughley. The designs that are common to both factories, such as 'parrot and fruit', 'fisherman' and many others, are never identical and were obviously re-designed and engraved for use at Caughley.

In the same year, 1774, Dr. Wall left Worcester to end his days at Bath. As he must have had such a lot to do with the success of the Company up to that time, it is right that a brief account be given of his life.

He was born in 1708 at Powick, a small village near Worcester; the exact date is not known but he was christened on October 19th. He took his degree of Bachelor of Medicine at Oxford in 1736 and lived and practised, very successfully, in Worcester from 1740 to 1774. As well as his interest in the porcelain works, he had a great deal to do with the development of the infirmary and a lane leading from his house in Foregate Street to the hospital was known for many years as Dr. Wall's Walk. A keen scientific investigator, he became well known in his day for such things as discovering the beneficial effects of Malvern waters and for his medical tracts on such subjects as lead poisoning arising from drinking cider from lead-glazed vessels. It could well be that his researches into lead poisoning led him into his experiments to find a fine porcelain.

As well as his medical and scientific work, he was a very keen and accomplished amateur artist. The Dyson Perrins Museum possesses a number of his paintings in oil and water colour, and his hand is noticeable on a number of pieces of porcelain (Plate 6). He also drew illustrations for J. Hervey's *Meditations and Contemplations*, 1748, and R. O. Cambridge's *The Scribbleraid*, 1751. He died at Bath on June 27th, 1776, and is buried in the Abbey, where there is a memorial tablet.

Dr. Wall had the distinction of having this early period of Worcester porcelain, from 1751 to 1783, named after him, turning him into the figurehead of the productions of this time. Many people refer to 'Dr. Wall porcelain' or the 'Dr. Wall period'; but both of these have recently become thought of as misnomers in view of the fact that Dr. Wall died in 1776. The period up to 1783 is now more usually referred to as the 'First Period', with the 'Flight' period taking over on the purchase of the factory by Thomas Flight in 1783.

Although it is doubtful if Dr. Wall had such an important effect on the day-to-day running of the factory as, say, William Davis, I think it is nevertheless wrong to dismiss him, with his great artistic and scientific bent, as of minor importance in the Company's success. If the excavation results show anything at all, it is now patently obvious that from, or about, the time that he left Worcester the productions of the factory changed.

It used to be thought that the period from 1751 to 1783 was one of continued high artistic perfection and that no change in policy was to be seen until the purchase by Thomas Flight. But it is now evident that there was a middle period from about 1776—the year of Dr. Wall's death—to about 1793, during which the products of the factory became much more commercially competitive. Whatever the cause, the effect seems to have led Worcester to enter the field of cheaper materials and printing in the 'willow pattern' style, with which the Caughley factory was enjoying such success.

The levels of this period in the excavation have produced the more simple ware of the late first period, 'willow pattern' type scenes previously thought of as Caughley type, and early Flight type ware all in one level—and all obviously being made at the factory at the same time. Why there was this change of policy into what might be referred to as the cheaper market is not clear, but it was probably purely a financial move made necessary by competition from Caughley and elsewhere. It is intriguing to wonder whether it would have occurred had Dr. Wall still been at the helm, but speculation on this can only be fruitless. It has been seen in many ceramic firms, however, that the retirement or death of a key figure—especially one who has been largely concerned in keeping up consistently high standards—can have a significant effect on production.

I put forward, tentatively, a new division into periods which seem to fit not only the dating sequences as shown by the excavation but also the death of Dr. Wall and the arrival of Martin Barr in 1793. These periods are:

Up to 1751 – Bristol period.
1751–1776 – Dr. Wall or First period.
1776–1793 – Davis/Flight or Middle period.
1793–1840 – Flight & Barr periods.

I realise that a certain amount of overlapping must take place. Bristol production seems to have gone on until the beginning of 1752, and with the same moulds being used often by the same workmen it is very difficult to tell whether some pieces are Bristol or Worcester: it will probably be best still to refer to these pieces as Bristol/Worcester. Then a large amount of ware of Dr. Wall type and decoration must still have gone on being made in the Davis/Flight period, especially ware needed as replacements—for it is virtually impossible to suddenly stop a particular shape or pattern which is in demand.

However one views the advisability of splitting the history of Worcester's production into periods, it must clearly be stated that the generally held view of a steady growth of one style and material—always very fine—from 1751 to 1783, and then a change to a simple style, developing again through the Flight period will have to be drastically rethought.

Reverting to the history of Warmstry House, in 1783 the complete factory was bought by Thomas Flight, who had previously acted as the Company's London agent at 2 Bread Street. The total cost was £3,000. Flight later took the shop of Mr. Bradley, the goldsmith at No. 33 High Street, opposite the

Guildhall, as a showroom; but in 1788 he moved to larger premises at No. 45 High Street.

It was to this latter shop that King George III and his family made a visit during their stay in the city to attend the Music Meeting (the Three Choirs Festival) in August 1788. Valentine Green refers to the visit in the following words:*

> On the afternoon of the same day, their Majesties and the Princesses . . . walked to Messrs. Flight & Barr's elegant china shop in High Street, where they remained almost an hour, and greatly admired the beautiful porcelain manufactured under the directing of those gentlemen and gave orders for an extensive assortment of it . . . and on the morning of Saturday, the ninth, their Majesties, the Princesses, and several of the nobility, went to the china factory, and saw the whole process of making china, at which they expressed great satisfaction and the King was pleased to leave ten pounds for the workmen.

In addition, the King granted his patent, allowing the Company to call itself 'Royal', and also suggested that they should open a shop in the West End of London, which led to the establishment at No. 1 Coventry Street. From this time onwards, a growing number of special services were made to the special order of various members of the Royal Family.

An interesting note in John Flight's diary† for July 19th, 1789, gives some idea of the difficulties that could still arise in the firing. He writes:

> Had a good deal of trouble last week about the Blue printing, the colours peel off in the burning-in and spoils a vast deal of ware. Every possible attention is payed to it to find out the cause and remedy it, but hitherto without success.

It is interesting to note the reference to blue printing, proving that the violet-blue printing of willow pattern scenes was still being done in 1789.

John Flight died in July 1791 and the business was continued by his son Joseph until Martin Barr was taken into partnership around 1793. Mr. Binns held that the year was 1793, although a piece bearing the mark Flight & Barr and dated 1792 is known. It seems likely that Barr was assisting Flight for some years before this time. From this date an incised B is frequently found on the ware, usually the only mark, that is thought to refer to the arrival of Martin Barr.

In 1807 Martin Barr, Junior, became a partner and the firm became known as Barr, Flight and Barr. The final change in the title of the firm came in 1813 when Martin Barr, Senior, died and his son George was taken into partnership, the title then becoming Flight, Barr and Barr, which it remained until 1840.

---

* *History and Antiquities of Worcester.* Note that the firm would not strictly have been known as 'Flight & Barr' at that time but as 'Flight's'.

† 'John Flight of Worcester', an article by Geoffrey Wills in *The Connoisseur*, June 1947.

Meanwhile, a breakaway factory had been started in Diglis (the site of the present factory) by Robert Chamberlain.

Valentine Green affirmed that Chamberlain had been the first apprentice at the Warmstry House factory and that 'the ornamental productions of the manufactory and the embellishment of the wares were carried on under the immediate direction of Mr. Chamberlain and his son for many years'.

By 1786 Chamberlain was engaged in decorating porcelain he bought in the white, either plain white glazed ware upon which he added decorations generally of a simple form of flowers and leaves in onglaze colours and gilding, or underglaze blue decorated, generally printed, which he either gilded or simply resold in his shop.

Most of this ware was bought from Thomas Turner's establishment at Caughley, as is proved from Chamberlain's own account books, still preserved by the Worcester Royal Porcelain Company Ltd. From the same books, however, it is clear that he also purchased ware from Flight, probably on the occasions when Turner was not able to supply him. I revert to this in Chapter III.

In 1788 the account books note the purchase of clay, which suggests that Chamberlain was making his first attempts at manufacturing, although for a year or so after that he still had occasion to buy ware in the white from Turner and Flight.

When Chamberlain's factory eventually reached the very high standard exemplified by the service made for Lord Nelson in 1802 and, later, the very fine body which he produced and called 'Regent China', he must have been a great rival to the Flight factory—although the latter kept up such a consistently high standard and attracted such a large number of orders for services that it too was able to prosper. The establishment of a third porcelain factory almost on the doorstep of the other works in 1801 by Thomas Grainger, who had married Robert Chamberlain's daughter, added to the competition, the three firms each having a shop and showroom in the same High Street.

It was not until 1840, however, that the Chamberlain and Flight factories finally amalgamated and most of the processes at Warmstry House were moved to Diglis, where the existing buildings were greatly enlarged. R. W. Binns described the amalgamation as a marriage of convenience and not of love,* and although we shall never know the full facts behind the merger, one of the main reasons may have been the greater suitability of the Diglis site. With the restricted space, difficult slope of ground and likelihood of flooding at Warmstry House, the move to Diglis, with plenty of land for expansion and bordered by the canal, must have seemed very attractive.

Warmstry House was still used by the new Company, now known as Chamberlain and Company, for the manufacture of 'encaustic' tiles—floor tiles made in the medieval style. Large quantities of these most interesting tiles were found on the site.

The tile-making business was sold to Messrs. Maw, who eventually went

* *A Century of Potting in the City of Worcester*, 1865.

to the Benthall Works near Ironbridge in Shropshire, and Warmstry House was bought by Dent's Gloves—gloving has long been one of the major industries of Worcester—who occupied the site for about 100 years until Worcester Corporation bought it. In 1960, the buildings were demolished and the site bulldozed to make way for the first two phases of the new Technical College, the main buildings of which stand where both Warmstry House and Mr. Holdship's new buildings once stood. The only landmarks from the eighteenth century which may still be seen are the Bishop's Palace on the South and the fine spire of St. Andrews to the North.

The old gardens of Warmstry House, once described as 'fair', at the time of writing serve as a rough car park between the Technical College and the river. But the Corporation plan, to be started when the college buildings are completed, will bring landscaped gardens back to Warmstry House again.

So the wheel will have come full circle. From a great house standing in its fair grounds, through its reign as the greatest porcelain factory in England, through its later use for tile and glove making and its present great role in the training of young people, this historic site will soon stand again in its fair gardens on the banks of the River Severn.

Chapter II

Warmstry House—The Excavation and Production Methods

An archaeological excavation can be described as a scientific investigation into the history of a site by carefully digging through all the levels of ground to the undisturbed subsoil. Levels build up through the natural accumulation of dirt and vegetation, or by the depositing of rubbish, or demolition of buildings by human hands.

It follows that each generation leaves its mark upon a site at its own particular level of occupation and that materials such as pottery and coins found in the lowest level are older than those in the level above it, and so on up to the highest and therefore the most recent level. Hence, it is very necessary when working down through these levels to keep the material found in each one separate from the others, so that the group of items in any one level can be taken as being from one period.

There are two complications that affect this ideal. Firstly, later generations can dig down through earlier levels in the form of pits, wells, building foundations etc., and these intrusions, as they are called, can cause later material to be deposited lower down in the ground than it would normally be; so the contents of pits and suchlike have to be cleared out first and kept separately, otherwise they can confuse the dating of the levels through which they have been cut. Secondly, only the latest dated pieces in a particular level can date it; for example, in your pocket or purse you might have half a dozen coins ranging from a Victorian one to one of this present year, but the presence of the Victorian coin does not mean that the group of coins was put in the pocket a hundred years ago. If a level is found with a fragment of Roman pottery and a medieval coin but the most recent object is a pipe bowl which can be dated about 1740, it is obvious that it was not until at least 1740 that those items came together in that level and that the Roman and medieval items do not date the level.

Archaeology has come a long way since the eighteenth and nineteenth centuries, when many ancient sites had great holes dug into them in the search for objects, the finding of pots or coins being the prime aim and no thought being given to recording the history of the site. Now, a tremendous amount can be learnt from a scientific investigation and nowhere can information be more important than from a kiln site. On such a site one naturally expects to discover quantities of wasters from the various making and firing stages—pots damaged or distorted and thrown away—and the shapes and designs thus found can be accepted as having been made on that site as wasters would not be brought from one factory to another.

In recent years, examination of the sites of a number of English eighteenth century porcelain factories has been possible—at Caughley, Liverpool and Lowestoft, for example—and the results have been far reaching. The opportunity of carrying out an excavation of the Warmstry House site in advance of development—one of many such sites in the city—was eagerly taken in order to investigate the factory levels and the probable line of the medieval and Roman defences lying beneath. Although a watch was kept on the higher part of the site when the Technical College was built across the position of Warmstry House and the original factory buildings that still remained, the circumstances of the mechanical excavation of the ground did not allow a scientific investigation. By the kindness of the contractors, a small amount of material was recovered by three members of the Royal Porcelain Company: Peter Ewence and Neal French, Company designers, and Cyril Shingler, the then Curator.

Although it was not possible to date any of the fragments found, as they were discovered quite haphazardly, the greatest benefit of the watching of the site was the tracing of a number of the original buildings, both those still standing and those remaining only under the ground. From this, it was clear that the description of the layout of the buildings given by Green and depicted in the print (Plate 3) was very accurate.

The decision to do an extensive excavation of the site in 1968 posed first the question of where to lay out the sixty-foot long, ten-foot wide trench that it was decided to dig. The area of Warmstry House itself was no longer available, covered up as it was by stage one of the Technical College; and stage two of the College covered 'Mr. Holdship's New Buildings'. The gardens of Warmstry House—where a number of the processes were set out running down Warmstry Slip—were in 1968 being used as a temporary rough car park, the surface of which had been formed by the dug out material from the College site being bulldozed across the area.

It was felt that the original open ground called in the early print the Coal Yard, running down to the river wall, would be the likeliest area to produce quantities of dumped wasters—the most helpful material to find in quantities. Accordingly, the trench was laid out from the river wall running due east; that is, up the originally sloping Warmstry House gardens.

The top three feet of rubble was dug out mechanically, as it was all disturbed material; but from there on, right down as far as the water table allowed, the remainder of the ground was carefully dug out entirely by hand, the material in each level being kept separately.

I must admit that, when we started, the enormous depths that the trench was to reach were not anticipated. As level after level was exposed—down through the working floors and foundations of Dent's glove factory; through levels containing Chamberlain's tiles; down to the Flight & Barr levels and the controversial Davis/Flight period; and then on into levels of the Dr. Wall period that got gradually earlier and earlier until, in the lowest ones, Bristol type pieces were found—the gradual unfolding of the history of Warmstry House had one so interested that it was not until the water table was struck below the thirteen-foot depth that the full realisation of the great rise in ground levels since 1751 really came upon us. Thirteen feet of accumulation is a fantastic amount if you visualise it as the height of a London double-decker bus.

Excavating at such great depths poses enormous problems in safety and also in the removal of the material out of the trench. Luckily, the sides of the trench—strengthened as they were by the walls and foundations of the glove factory and by the large number of floor levels that had been built across the site at different times in an attempt to level up the steeply-sloping ground—did not once collapse in any way, even through some of the worst excavating weather that I have known, when not only a summer snowstorm but also prolonged wet weather and a flooded River Severn left floodwater actually in the trench up to a height of seven feet on two separate occasions. For the easier removal of spoil from the bottom of the trench, an ingenious modern application of an ancient Egyptian principle of drawing water out of a river was used. And it worked very well, if rather primitively.

But not even the most ingenious device could enable us to beat the worst enemy encountered, which was the water table level at the thirteen-foot mark with obviously still many more feet of occupation levels to go through. The raising of the level of the river by the building of the locks in the Victorian period had put these earliest levels beyond possible reach; too elaborate a pumping system would have been needed than was possible. We had to be grateful that, at any rate, there were all the factory levels laid out for our inspection. Following a plan of the site (Fig. 2), a simplified drawing of the factory levels can be seen in Figure 3.

In Figure 3 the main levels have been numbered from one—the disturbed top soil—to eight—the earliest Bristol/Worcester level. Fragments illustrated in this book have the level in which they were found shown. You will therefore be able to see at a glance from which level they have come and form your own opinion about the sequence of the development of shape and decoration. Some patterns and shapes obviously were very popular and had a long life, and where these are found in more than one level this is indicated. Level One contains disturbed materials that might have come from anywhere on the site at any time, so that close dating is not possible. Such fragments are shown because they are either the only ones of their kind to be found or are more suitable for illustration than pieces found in definite levels. In all cases, the level in which the fragment illustrated appears is shown first—generally the level in which most of the same types occur—followed by other levels in which similar fragments were found.

From a study of the simplified plan, I am sure you will get a good picture

of the incredible original slope of the site from the way in which most of the
levels tend to dip sharply towards the river. An occasional flood that washed
over the site has left its mark in the debris of sand and shingle remaining; and
an emergency wall built of large curved bricks from a demolished kiln and a
big embankment of sand raised to keep the flood out point to the great trouble
they must have had from that source.

No trace was found of the original sandstone wall that formed the riverside
boundary of the factory. This had been replaced, early in the nineteenth century, by the still surviving brick wall.

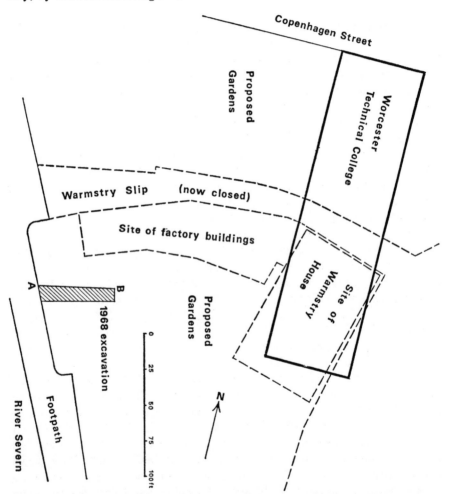

Fig. 2. A plan of Warmstry House site at the beginning of 1969. The continuous
line represents boundaries and buildings in existence at that date. The broken line
represents boundary lines and buildings destroyed in levelling work prior to the
construction of the Worcester Technical College. Letters A–B represent the line of
the excavation, which can be referred to the plan on the next page. Anyone visiting
the site will be able to find the line of the excavation by projecting the right hand
corner of the Technical College towards the river footpath.

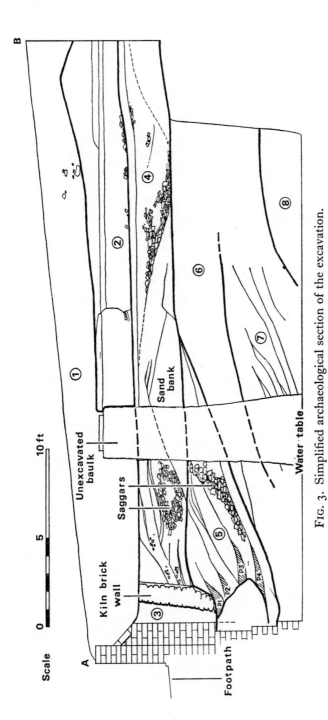

FIG. 3. Simplified archaeological section of the excavation.

The finding of ware in the biscuit stage has provided an opportunity of examining techniques of manufacture that are no longer clear when the ware has been covered with glaze and fired again. And the finding of kiln furniture —such as saggars, supports and props—and even workmen's tools has helped enormously to make clear the manufacturing stages that were previously imperfectly understood or only guessed at. For those who are unfamiliar with the processes, there follows a fairly simple explanation of what they were and how they were carried out at Warmstry House in the eighteenth century, as proved by a close examination of the material found, using some of the technical terms that are current now in the Worcester factory, a number of which are of considerable antiquity.

The method of making shapes seems to have been confined to throwing and pressing, used separately or in conjunction.

Throwing is, I suppose, the most widely known way of making pots. It is the traditional method; and even today, when at least in industrial ceramics it is used less and less, most people still assume that all pots are made by throwing. For an eighteenth century porcelain factory, it held great advantages. It is quick, produces little waste of material and, most important, requires no moulds. Moulds were and are a considerable nuisance to potters: they are difficult and expensive to produce, heavy to carry about the factory, bulky to store, and at least in the case of plaster moulds have a very limited working life. Throwing is the ideal way of making cups, bowls, jugs, teapots and coffee pots—in fact, any vessel having a round section and not needing any surface modelling. The method, briefly, is as follows.

A ball of plastic porcelain clay is thrown on to the revolving wheel-head by the potter and centred by pressure from the heel of his right hand. Having worked the clay up and down a couple of times with both hands to get it to the right consistency, all the time using water as a lubricant, the potter presses the tips of the fingers of his left hand down into the ball of clay to form a hollow. Then, with right hand outside and left hand within, he exerts pressure on the clay and it rises to form the wall of the pot. The shape and section of the pot are alike governed by the two hands working together as a single tool. More than one throw may be necessary to achieve the final shape—but the fewer the better, as at this stage the clay is very weak and may well collapse if worked too much. Cut from the wheel-head with a wire, the pot is allowed to dry to a 'leather' hardness and is fitted over a wooden lump or 'chum' on a horizontal lathe so that it can be turned to its final shape. Surplus clay is turned from the revolving pot with a sharp metal tool; the foot-ring is shaped, and the tool skims lightly over the whole outside surface of the pot to give it its characteristic smooth finish and fine section.

For a very tall vessel, such as the huge vase in the Dyson Perrins Museum of 27 inches in height, more than one session would be necessary. First the potter would throw the base up to a limit of fifteen inches or so and allow the vessel to dry sufficiently to withstand an extra amount of clay being added in the form of a sausage pressed around the rim. The extra clay thus added would then be thrown up a further distance, the process being repeated until the desired height is achieved. The tall vase referred to is formed of three such separate throws: these can be felt quite clearly from the inside, where the junctions were made.

On some vessels with a basically round section but where modelled decoration is required—such as a fluted bowl or a cup with embossed modelling like the 'chrysanthemum' pattern (Plate 87)—a variation of throwing known as 'jollying' is used. For this process, a mould of the outside shape of the pot is needed. An assistant first throws a 'liner' or small thick cylinder of clay of the right weight. This is placed inside the revolving mould; and the potter's left hand, as when throwing, forms the inside of the vessel while the mould does the work of his right hand and forms the outside complete with modelled decoration. The inside section is corrected by a slate profile and the pot is allowed to dry out to leather hardness, when the foot-ring is turned exactly as on thrown pieces. This method, in a slightly mechanised version, is still in use at Worcester and is the best and least expensive way of making cups and small bowls.

Small plates and saucers are made by an 'inside out' version of this method. A mould is made of the inside shape of the piece—plain or with modelling, as required—and on to it is thrown a flat round 'bat' of clay. The bat is prepared by roughly flattening a ball of clay on a slate or marble topped bench by hand and then banging it with a heavy flat round tool made of plaster and 'pitcher' (fired clay) called a 'maw'. The bat is pressed down on to the revolving mould with hand and sponge, and the back shape is achieved with a hand-held pitcher profile. Later, the foot-ring is turned to its final shape—probably before removal from the mould.

These first three methods require the use of a turntable or wheel-head turning at some speed in order to be effective—the motive power probably being supplied by an apprentice pedalling or turning a handle to drive the wheel-head. The remaining methods make use of a turntable merely to help and speed up the process. This is an important distinction. The preceding methods are all variations of the throwing technique, with the mould playing rather a secondary role. But from now on, the mould takes over and the following processes are all forms of pressing.

On large hollow-ware pieces of round section but modelled on the outside and of a size or shape unsuitable for jollying, a liner would be prepared, placed in the mould and pressed up against it with a sponge, the potter slowly revolving the mould to ensure even pressure and thickness. Mask jugs and such things as fluted teapots would have been made this way, some of them press moulded in two- or three-piece moulds. The join marks can sometimes be seen.

From this, it is an easy step to oval section pieces like sauce-boats and tureens. The only difference is that the liner would not be thrown but an oval one made by placing a bat of clay on a cloth over an oval former or chum and forming it to the rough shape before placing it in the mould. The point of the cloth is merely to facilitate handling. This way of producing a liner is still in use at the factory, for making oval casseroles.

This leaves only the factory's great variety of oval and irregular-shaped trays and dishes to account for. These are made, as with saucers, over a mould called a 'hump', which forms the inside of the piece. A bat of clay is made and laid over the hump and pressed down and into every crevice with hand and sponge. If a footring is required—and on most small pieces it is left off—a roll of clay is pressed on and formed to the correct section with a pitcher profile. This is another method still in use at the factory, in this case in absolutely unchanged form.

These various processes explain the two methods referred to by Valentine Green (see page 10) when he mentions pressing by hand and on a wheel, the wheel being used by the workman to assist in obtaining smoothness and symmetry and which might be simply a turntable and not necessarily a potter's wheel. They also explain the reference in the price list (page 8) to 'milk jugs round and pressed', the round ones being simply thrown vessels and the pressed ones formed in a mould from a liner.

After the completed article has partly dried into a leather-hard state, it needs to be turned like the ordinary thrown ware and 'fettled' or cleaned up before being set aside to dry. At this stage, also, handles and spouts are put on.

The ware is then ready for firing in the biscuit kiln. But before considering this process, a few words about the moulds themselves might be apposite. The only early moulds found on the site were in 'pitcher'—that is, fired clay. One of the big surprises of the excavation was that no trace was found of plaster-of-Paris moulds of an early period. The only plaster mould was found during the College excavation—a 'Blind Earl' cup mould—and this could be from the Flight & Barr period or later.

There are considerable differences in the making and use of plaster and pitcher moulds. For example, the present-day method of mould-making in plaster involves a model of the piece being prepared in hard plaster, or some other material, one sixth larger than the intended size to allow for shrinkage of the body during firing. (Although a reduction of a sixth may not sound a great deal, it actually results in a loss of close on fifty per cent of volume.) A mould is carefully made from this in plaster, keeping in mind the fact that not only one piece is to be made from it but also subsequent moulds. This first mould is known as the 'block' mould and it is used just to cast the first two or three samples. If these turn out satisfactorily, moulds are then made of each piece of the block mould: these 'positive' pieces are called 'block case' moulds. From them could be produced 'working' moulds. But such is the need to insure them against damage that they are generally used only to produce 'working case' moulds via a second-generation block mould. It is from working case moulds that production working moulds in quantity are made. A very elaborate process, the complications of which are partially made necessary by the short working life of plaster.

If we work on the assumption that the eighteenth century Worcester potters used plaster only for special moulds—notably large ones—and used pitcher or fired earthenware for the bulk of their production, then their method might have been as follows, based upon examination of the pitcher moulds found.

A sauce-boat, for instance, would be modelled roughly, with little or no ornament—and considerably oversize, to allow not only for the shrinkage of the porcelain vessel but also for that of the pitcher mould. A mould in clay would be taken off this and, when dried to leather hardness, the decoration would be engraved into the surface of the mould in reverse. This would have to be done afresh for each working mould and would account for the great number of clearly similar but not identical sauce-boats and like vessels of that period. The working life of pitcher moulds is enormous compared with that of plaster ones, thus making the large number of separate and different working moulds a reasonable proposition.

Pitcher seems also to have been used when case moulds of present-day types were required—as, for example, for cups. The basic outside shape of the cup would be turned on the wheel and, when leather hard, decoration would be carved on it. It seems likely that where pitcher cases were in use plaster moulds would be made from them, the use of pitcher for block, case and mould possibly putting an unreasonable strain on the modeller in ascertaining the actual size of model required to give him a final piece of the correct size.

If pitcher was used as the original model for each piece that required a plaster mould, and the model was made in such a way that it could be used as a case mould, then the whole system of blocks, block cases, working cases, etc., could be short circuited, as the life of a pitcher model was endless. Cup moulds could be made using the model and a flat base as the case, and more complicated pieces could be made by using the model and parts of old moulds to produce new ones. Although this is difficult technically, it is a method still used today on some pieces.

The piece having been made, turned, and a handle and spout put on where necessary, it was ready for its first or biscuit firing. This was carried out in the biscuit kiln at a temperature probably not much over 1,000° Centigrade. In experiments carried out on some underfired pieces from the site, it has become apparent that the body fired at a fantastically low temperature. Obviously, the greatest danger is during the first firing, when the object is turned from raw material into a fully fused and vitrified piece of porcelain. Proof of this is shown by the fact that the greater proportion of wasters found on the site were biscuit ones. The stresses during the first firing, when the ware shrinks in size, are very great; and the fact that the vast majority of the biscuit wasters were not badly distorted and had very few firing defects shows how magnificent the recipe was.

One of the extraordinary features of the biscuit firing was that open bowl shapes—such as tea bowls—could be fired stacked up inside each other without any protective material, such as alumina powder, to stop them sticking together. Yet very few bowls were actually found stuck together, proving what an extraordinarily fine body the factory had to work with; for it is difficult to fire earthenware in this way, and almost inconceivable that porcelain could be thus treated.

The pieces were then put into 'saggars'—suitably shaped highly fired clay protective containers made in one of the departments of the factory—which protected the ware from the flames of the kiln and kept them clean. None of the saggars found on the site had any pieces stuck to them—additional proof of the very fine porcelain body used. Some of the pieces which might be in danger of distorting at the rim during the reduction in firing were placed upon shaped clay supports which kept the rim true. This was particularly necessary for hors d'œuvre sets (Plate 93), the problem being that the trays had to fit carefully with each other in groups around a centre. Special shaped supports to hold these in perfect shape were found.

The packed saggars were then stacked up in the great biscuit kiln, which was sealed up and fired by coal, the firing lasting for a number of days. When finally the kiln was opened, the fully fired ware was examined, the wasters were discarded, and the perfect pieces were ready for their next stage.

If a piece was intended for simple underglaze cobalt blue painting or printing, or if cobalt was to form part of the decoration of an item which would be finished off with further onglaze enamel colours—as, for example, blue scale or some of the Oriental type patterns—it would go on to the decoration rooms. Both underglaze painting and printing were carried out direct on to the biscuit body. Painting was done with cobalt oxide in the form of smalt—a fused mixture of cobalt oxide, sand and a flux, which was mixed with water and normally used in two strengths, the lighter one being painted on first and then touched up with the darker. When the blue was part of an onglaze pattern, such as the 'fan' or the 'Queen Charlotte', the colour was just a flat application of the darker strength (see Plate 50). At this stage, the painter's mark or the factory mark of the crescent, 'W' or fretted square would be put on the base by the painter.

Transfer printing from designs engraved or etched on copper plates is another process which has remained virtually unchanged since the eighteenth century. At the present Worcester factory, it is done as follows.

The ceramic colour is mixed on a heated metal plate, called a 'backstone', with a medium known as 'printer's oil', prepared from oils, tar, pitch and lead boiled together. The engraved copper is also placed on the backstone and the mixed colour is transferred to it with a flat knife, or 'spud', and forced into every part of the design with a blunt piece of wood, or 'dabber'. The surplus colour is removed carefully and returned to the backstone. The copper is taken from the heat and, while cooling, a 'boss' made of corduroy with tow filling is used to remove any scum from it. This leaves the surface clean and shining, while the engraved or etched lines are full of colour.

The transfer paper is bathed in 'prime'—a mixture of soft soap and water—and laid on the copper, which has been placed on the 'plank' of the press. The press resembles a mangle with large diameter rollers between which is a thick sheet of metal which moves with the rollers as they are turned: this is the plank. Covered with smooth flannel, the copper and the transfer paper are rolled through the press and back once. Then the paper print is carefully peeled off the copper over a gentle heat. Meanwhile, the article to be decorated has been prepared by being coated with a varnish and allowed to cool.

The transfer print, which has been trimmed to shape with scissors, is placed on the vessel in the required position and rubbed on firmly. The transfer paper is gently washed off and the pattern, which has adhered to the varnish, is cleaned up prior to firing.

Both painted and printed pieces, as also those involving combinations of the two, were then 'hardened' on in the cooler part of the 'glost' kiln—the term for the kiln in which the glaze is fired. The reason for doing this before the piece was actually glazed was to fuse the decoration to the biscuit and reduce the chance of it running with the molten glaze. Besides ensuring a crisp decoration, it also ensured that the vegetable oils in the colour would be burnt away and not contaminate the glaze.

A considerable quantity of this hardened-on decorated ware was found, especially in four pits, the earliest of about 1760 and the latest of about 1770. It has proved most instructive in understanding the techniques of painting and printing, as the decoration was not covered up or blurred by the glaze. Most of the decorated fragments shown in the illustrations are in this form; and those who see unglazed cobalt pieces for the first time have great difficulty in recognising the strange black or browny-black colour for the same pigment which the effects of glaze and a further firing are going to transform into the typical and beautiful Worcester blue.

It seems to me probable that the famous Worcester scale blue grounds were carried out in much the same sequence as other underglaze blue painting. First the reserved panels would be drawn in outline, then the blue areas would be washed in with the weaker of the two strengths of cobalt oxide. When this was dry, the scale pattern would be painted on over the ground in the heavier strength. With the mark added, the piece would be hardened on in the normal way.

Proof that the hardening on was done in the glost kiln (at a probable temperature of just under 1,000° Centigrade) was provided by the finding of a large number of unglazed fragments in which the cobalt had partly or fully turned blue through the 'flashing over' of the glaze during the firing from some of the glazed pieces in the kiln. During the glost firing, volatile glaze is present in the air of the kiln and can cause troubles like this.

Assuming that the hardened-on blue-painted pieces came through this firing satisfactorily, they were then ready—together with the plain biscuit pieces—for glazing.

Glazing was generally done by holding a piece between finger and thumb, or with the assistance of a wire to avoid too many fingermarks on it, and dipping it into the bucket of glaze, swirling it round to spread the glaze evenly, shaking off the surplus and then putting it aside to dry.

When the pieces were dry, they were all examined before being put into the glost kiln to make sure that there was no danger of the glaze running down the feet of the vessels and sticking them to the kiln.

When glaze fuses, it spreads to a small extent, flowing slightly over the more curving parts of a vessel. A particularly dangerous area was the foot, where, if there was too much raw glaze, it was possible for that on the inside of the foot-ring to begin to flow during firing and draw the surplus on the inside of the base after it—thus building up a substantial quantity which could run down the foot and stick the vessel to the kiln furniture. This was frequently avoided by wiping surplus glaze away from the lower part of the foot-ring with a sponge or by taking out the glaze lying in the inside of the foot-ring with a pointed stick or metal implement. Either method accounts for the very common effect of a glaze-free margin* just inside the foot—usually an irregular line running around the foot which leaves the area in the angle of the foot and the base free of glaze.

The glaze-free margin is often incorrectly referred to as 'glaze shrinkage' or 'retreating glaze'; but as already explained, glaze flows when fusing and does not retreat or shrink. A large number of fragments covered with raw (unfired) glaze were found on the site—pieces probably dropped or damaged after being dipped—and some of them, but not all, show the glaze-free margin quite clearly scored in the foot.

This process of clearing raw glaze from danger spots is still employed in the Worcester factory—yet another example of the many processes that remain unchanged over 200 years—and is referred to as 'pegging'. It would not be surprising if this term, which a worker at the factory had passed on to him when he was a youngster, was the actual eighteenth century one, as the task could have been done with a pointed wooden peg. Now, however, the pegging is done with a broken pen-nib and is confined to clearing away excess of raw glaze from around embossed flowers so that the flowing glaze does not cover up the modelling of the flowers. It also prevents pooling and bubbling of the glaze, which can occur quite easily on present-day glaze, which would appear to flow much more freely than that of the eighteenth century. It is nowadays found that the glaze flows back over the pegging line, covering it up; and it is possible that a number of early Worcester pieces that do not show a glaze-free margin had, in fact, been pegged but the glaze had re-covered the raw line. It is not necessary, nowadays, to peg the foot as the glaze is sprayed on much more evenly than is possible by dipping. Some pieces which were covered with raw, unfired glaze have been refired in the present Company's glost kilns and the glaze fused perfectly, turning the cobalt blue even after two hundred years in the ground.

When the ware had been fired in the glost kiln, the fully decorated under-glaze-blue pieces and those that were intended for disposing in the white, as undecorated glazed ware is called, would be sent to the despatch department for transmission by road and river. The remainder, earmarked for onglaze decoration, went forward to the painting or printing departments.

One of the disappointments of the excavation was that only a handful of onglaze decorated pieces was found. This was not really unexpected. Usually, very few pieces of this nature are found on a kiln site—mainly because there were, of course, fewer chances of anything going wrong with the pieces in the lower firing temperatures of the decorating kilns; and also greater care was

---

* This feature is not, as is often believed, unique to the Worcester porcelain. It is to be found on most Caughley porcelain and on some pieces from other factories.

taken that these pieces, which had involved the outlay of so much money to bring them to this stage, should not be damaged. In addition, as explained, we had chosen an area which would have been rough ground, nearly a hundred yards away from the decorating rooms.

Onglaze printing was carried out in the same way as underglaze except that the colour was enamel and was fired on the glaze, remaining partly on the surface of the vessel. The majority of pieces were printed in a strong black—known in their own time as 'jet enamels'—although lilac and purple are less common variants. The Perrins Museum possesses a number of the original copper plates (a 'pull' from one of them—'The draw-well'—is shown in Plate 36), and they are very beautiful objects in their own right.

As well as straightforward black transfers, prints could be tinted in, or washed over, in enamel colours (Plate 35) or printed in outline and the colours filled in. It is thought that this latter process was to enable effective coloured pieces to be produced by inexperienced painters—possibly young boys or girls—and it might be likened to a child's painting book where an outline is filled in by numbers. Some people argue, on the evidence that Giles purchased a relatively small quantity of this ware at several sales in London, that the outline prints all went to Giles' decorating studios for filling in. But this seems to me extraordinary when it would have been easy to find young apprentices in plenty at the factory to do such simple work. Outline filling in is a technique that Worcester and other factories have employed at most periods, and there is no reason to suppose that it was not done in eighteenth century Worcester, even if no actual proof of this was found.

The other form of onglaze decoration was hand painting in enamels, which ranges from the early copies of Chinese painting and the Meissen type of flower painting to the more mature and typical great paintings on the scale blue pieces in the panels left white by the underglaze scale painters—the onglaze ground colours of yellow, green, claret, etc., probably inspired and later done by the Chelsea migrants—to the later Dr. Wall simpler patterns of gold and puce, leading into the Davis/Flight era of simple sprigs of flowers in gold.

Some of these more splendid coloured pieces involved a number of decorating firings, made necessary because of some painters' techniques whereby the basic underlying colours were first fired and then strengthened before a second firing. This can be seen very clearly in a most interesting vase in the Perrins Museum, painted by the great Scottish painter John Donaldson, which had probably 'fled' and been damaged during its first firing, so that the second painting and subsequent refiring were not proceeded with.

Finally, after the requisite number of decorating firings, the gilders applied the gold—scraping it off a block of the material, mixing it with honey to make it flow, and applying it by brush. The piece then had to be refired at the lowest temperature of all to fuse the gold and drive out the honey medium. After this firing, the gold had to be 'burnished' with an agate or with fine silver sand to bring up the brightness.

To sum up the foregoing complicated procedures: a piece is made and then fired in the biscuit kiln at its highest temperature, where it turns into fully vitrified porcelain in a biscuit state. If the piece is decorated underglaze in cobalt, the colour has to be hardened on in the cooler part of the glost kiln. Then the ware is glazed and fired in the glost kiln, which fuses the glaze at a lower temperature than the biscuit kiln. The piece then proceeds, if necessary, to its onglaze decoration—the enamel colours needing to be fired at least once in a decorating kiln, again at a lower temperature than the glost. If gilding is applied, the piece is refired at an even lower temperature.

As this summary makes clear, at each successive firing the temperature is lower, so that no damage is done to the previous fired work—the only exception being the hardening on process, where the subsequent glazing is fired at a slightly higher temperature. (This led to some difficulties in the early years, for the cobalt blue ran and became blurred.)

The overriding impression gained from the excavations is of the wonderful quality of the raw material that was used at the factory. Very little bad distortion or making troubles have been noticed; and bodies which could be treated as theirs were—bowls fired in stacks; body walls sometimes eggshell thin— together with their ability for making and controlling such difficult little pieces as the hors d'œuvres trays, which had to fit into each other after firing, certainly explains the great regard in which Worcester ware was, and still is, held.

Even though the long-held beliefs about the recognition of early Worcester by translucency and shape of foot-ring can no longer be valid, there is one old axiom by which eighteenth century Worcester may still be judged: its craze-free glaze. For except for a couple of fragments that had probably dropped into the firebox and had their surface destroyed, none was found with any crazing. So one of the classic ways by which Worcester has always been recognised remains as true today as in the past—although it must be made clear that some other factories, notably Caughley, also had craze-free glaze.

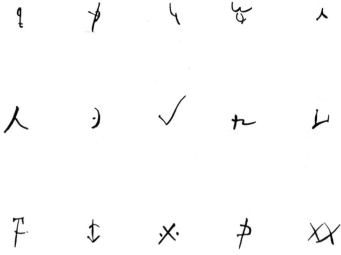

DRAWING OF PAINTERS' MARKS FOUND ON WARMSTRY HOUSE SITE WASTERS

Colour Plate I. Large flower or bulb pot of hexagonal
shape, painted in underglaze cobalt blue of a shade typical
of early Dr. Wall Period blue and white, in alternating
panels of bird and flower scenes. The rim is painted with
a cell border pattern. The pot is shown standing in a fragment of an unglazed site waster (level 7) of the correct
shallow hexagonal stand in which the pot, which has a
drainage hole in its base, should rest. Height of pot, 10½
inches, height of stand, 2½ inches; mark, painted open
crescent, under pot; c. 1757–60.

1.   Examples of marks found on the site, all of them in underglaze-blue and photographed from the actual wasters.

   Row 1: Painters' marks.

   Row 2: Two forms of the 'W' mark, a scratch cross and a typical painted crescent.

   Row 3: Three different versions of the square mark. Many other arrangements were found.

   Row 4: A mark copied from the Chinese, and two marks based on the Meissen crossed swords.

   Row 5: Printed crescent marks, found on printed ware. The third from the left is generally found as a hatched crescent and might rarely be found with the addition of a man-in-the-moon.

   Row 6: Disguised Chinese numerals, showing two different forms of '2', a '4', a '5', a '7' and an '8'.

2. A group of five pieces marked 'Bristol' or 'Bristoll'. The figure of the Chinaman (height, $6\frac{3}{4}$ inches) also has the date '1750' embossed on his back. The sauce-boat on the left (length, $6\frac{3}{4}$ inches), in underglaze-blue, was painted by the 'three-dot' painter, and the one on the right (length, $7\frac{1}{2}$ inches) was left in the white. Both cream-boats are painted in under-glaze-blue. The one on the right is $2\frac{1}{8}$ inches high; the one on the left is $4\frac{1}{2}$ inches long, and the word 'Bristoll' may be seen under the foot. A fragment from level 8 on the site, identical with the base of the latter cream-boat but not having a mark, is also shown. The five finished pieces c. 1750–52 (Page 32).

3 (*opposite, above*). An engraving from *The Gentleman's Magazine* of 1752, the editor of which was Edward Cave, one of the fifteen original partners of the Worcester Porcelain Company. This is the earliest illustra-tion of the factory, a year after its foundation. The only building still standing is St. Andrew's Church, the fine spire of which is shown (No. 1). It was outside the area marked No. 9—the coal yard—that the excavation was done (Page 7).

4 (*opposite*). A view of the factory, in about 1758, drawn and engraved by Robert Hancock. The building on the left is the one marked No. 3 on the 1752 engraving—the biscuit kilns; the one behind it is No. 4, the glost kiln; and the kiln above this is No. 5. The small building to the right above No. 5 is the pressing and modelling gallery, No. 6. Above these, at the top of the hill, lies Warmstry House itself. Hancock seems to have altered the actual arrangement of the house in order to make a better picture and to give full effect to the masts of the boat (Page 18).

THE
PORCELAIN MANUFACTORY
at WORCESTER.

The River Severn

J. D. delin.

J. C. sculp.

EXPLANATION.

1 St Andrews. 2 Warmsley flip. 3 Biscuit kilns. 4 Glasing kilns. 5 Great kiln for segurs. 6 Pressing and modelling gallery.—— 7 Rooms for throwing, turning, and stove drying the ware on the first floor *a*, of the chamber floors. 8 The garden. 9 The yard for coals. 10 Mr Evett's house and garden, landlord of the premises. *b* The eight windows in two large chambers, in which the ware is placed on stallions, on the East and North, where are the painters rooms.——All the beginning of the process is carried on under the quadrangular building ground floor, mark'd A; in its N. W. angle is the great sowl and ring; in the N. E. the horses turn the same, and the levigators near to the rowl. The next (on the ground floor) is the flip and treading rooms, behind Number 4 is the glasing room, behind 5 is the secret room on the ground floor.

N. B. A sale of this manufacture will begin at the *Worcester* music meeting, on *Sept.* 20, with great variety of ware, and, 'tis laid, at a moderate price.

3

4

5. A cream-boat of Bristol/Worcester type with a moulded scene of a Chinese pavilion and bushy trees behind fencing that runs uphill towards the top of the handle. It is decorated around the inside of the rim with sprays of flowers in onglaze enamels and is similar to the one marked 'Wigornia' under the foot. The waster from the site (level 8) is not identical but is from a similar pitcher mould and, being unglazed, shows the modelling very clearly. The painter's mark is inside the base. Height, $2\frac{1}{2}$ inches; c. 1752–58 (Page 31).

6. A mug of Bristol/Worcester type with spreading base, painted in onglaze enamels with scenes representing 'Conquest' and 'Gratitude' on each side. In the front, opposite the handle, is an inscribed monument referring to the Worcester Parliamentary Election of 1747. The type of painting is very similar to that on several oil and water-colour paintings by Dr. John Wall in the Dyson Perrins Collection, and it is reasonably certain that the mug was also painted by him. Height, $3\frac{5}{8}$ inches; mark: incised saltire cross, underneath the base (Page 36).

7. Bristol/Worcester type cup with a fluted body, the flutes ending in a wavy crenellated shape near the rim, decorated with small sprays of flowers and a border in onglaze enamels. At the left is a waster from the site (level 8) of exactly matching shape. Height, $2\frac{1}{10}$ inches; c. 1752–58 (Page 34).

8. Bristol/Worcester tea bowl and saucer, twelve-sided, concavely fluted, scalloped edge, painted in onglaze enamels with birds and flowering prunus and formal border. Also shown are exactly matching unglazed wasters (level 7). Diameter of saucer, $3\frac{3}{4}$ inches; diameter of bowl, $2\frac{1}{2}$ inches; c. 1752–58 (Page 34).

9. A tall vase of Bristol/Worcester type decorated in the 'famille verte' style with Chinamen and dragons, the vessel showing the distortion of shape frequently seen on the taller Worcester pieces. Height, 9 inches; c. 1750–55.

10. Bristol/Worcester teapot and cover and a waster fragment (level 7) of fluted shape, decorated in the panels in underglaze-blue with delft-type scenes of a Chinaman fishing from a punt. The pot is of squat shape with a round handle, the cover having a very deep octagonal neck and flange. The knob is of button mushroom shape, which is also found at the same period with a depressed ring at the top instead of a point. Height, 5 inches; c. 1752–58 (Page 34).

11. Bristol/Worcester teapot and cover, vertically fluted, very finely decorated in onglaze enamels in the Bristol delft-style with a Chinese man with long talon fingers in an attitude as if 'calling a flock of birds'. Height, 6 inches; c. 1752–58.

12. Bristol/Worcester type bowl with eight wide vertical flutes from rim to foot, decorated in onglaze enamels in the 'famille verte' style with flowering branches growing from rocks. Diameter, 8 inches; c. 1750–58.

13. Pair of small vases of baluster shape with curious handles, painted in onglaze enamels with, on one side, a standing Chinaman holding what appears to be a basket of plants and, on the other, a large vase and a flowering plant. These shapes are found decorated in both Bristol/Worcester and early Worcester styles. Height, 6½ inches; c. 1750–58.

14. Two mugs of Bristol/Worcester type with spreading base and strap handle, the curved end cut sharp away. Painted underglaze with a 'Long Eliza' figure holding a book, in a landscape with triangle-shaped fences, flowers and a rocky island in the distance on one side, and on the other a fence, rocks, a willow tree and battleship turrets in the distance. Two unglazed fragments from the site (level 7) of exactly matching shape and decoration are shown. Height, 3½ and 3 3/10 inches; c. 1750–56.

15. Two teacups of Bristol/Worcester type, each with elaborate scrolled handle and four flutes narrowing from the top to the bottom, shown with an unglazed waster (level 7) exactly matching the shape. The cup on the left is decorated underglaze with a Chinese lady holding a fan, sprays of flowers in alternating panels. The cup on the right is decorated in onglaze enamels with a 'Long Eliza' figure carrying a sunshade in a landscape, the alternate panels with flowers. Height, $2\frac{1}{2}$ inches; c. 1752–56.

16. Three Bristol/Worcester type pieces: an octagonal fluted tea bowl decorated with onglaze flowers; a small hexagonal fluted vase, decorated onglaze with flowering prunus growing from a rock; and a cream jug decorated onglaze with a crane-like bird in a flowering landscape. Height of vase, $4\frac{1}{2}$ inches; c. 1752–56.

17. Two thrown bottles, the finished one on the right having a straight neck and the unglazed waster on the left (pit 4) having a flaring neck. Both are very finely painted by the same hand with a scene of fishermen, boatmen, a rocky island with a willow tree joined to another island by a bridge, and 'crazy' birds in the sky. The waster shows clearly the magnificent quality of the painting. Height of finished bottle, $10\frac{3}{4}$ inches; c. 1760–65.

18. Magnificent tureen and cover with elaborate moulded floral-decoration panels and a curving dolphin on the cover. The two handles are pressed. A fragment of an identical biscuit waster (level 6) is shown. Very finely decorated underglaze, with figure scenes in the main panels and elaborate trailing floral sprays. Height to top of cover, $8\frac{1}{2}$ inches; length, $17\frac{1}{2}$ inches; c. 1753–58.

19. Detail of a panel on the cover of the large tureen shown in the previous plate, which well illustrates the superb modelling and painting of these fine early pieces. Length of panel, $4\frac{1}{2}$ inches.

20. A finger-bowl stand, painted underglaze-blue with the early 'fisherman and cormorant' pattern, shown with a glazed waster (level 6) of a finger-bowl of matching pattern. Notice the particular nicked arrangement of the rim. Diameter of stand, $5\frac{9}{10}$ inches; mark: painter's mark like an 'R'; c. 1753–58.

21. Water jug and basin, finely painted in underglaze-blue with a scene with fishermen and boatmen. Also shown is a waster (level 5) matching the jug foot. Border number 20 is only found on special pieces of the larger variety. Height, $8\frac{3}{4}$ inches; diameter, $10\frac{1}{2}$ inches; marks: on jug, script 'W'—on basin, open crescent; c. 1758–65.

22. Bowl of early Worcester type, painted in underglaze-blue with a landscape of two islands—a house on each—rocks in the water, border number 8 inside. Also, an unglazed waster (level 5) painted by the same hand. Diameter, $4\frac{1}{10}$ inches; mark: a painter's mark on both pieces, as shown on the waster; c. 1753–58.

23. Sauce-boat of early Worcester type, the modelling of which can vary in many small details from piece to piece. Painted in underglaze-blue with Chinese-type scenes in panels and floral sprays in the delft style. Length, $7\frac{1}{4}$ inches; mark: a decorator's mark like a swastika; c. 1754–58 (Page 25).

24. Bowl, painted in underglaze-blue with a 'precipice' scene: two houses seemingly built on a precipice. On the other side of the bowl, a bridge joins two islands on which there are houses. A lozenge border inside (border number 8). On the left is an unglazed waster of a similar-sized bowl (pit 4) of the same pattern but by a different painter. Many differences in technique may be observed. Diameter $8\frac{1}{2}$ inches; mark: open painted crescent; c. 1760–65.

25. Mug of cylindrical shape with a strap handle, painted in underglaze-blue with a long Chinese female figure, a little boy to her right, landscape with trees and three long-tailed birds. The unglazed waster (level 5) of the same pattern provides an opportunity to see the high quality of painting technique unfortunately usually blurred by the glost firing. Height, 6 inches; mark: open painted crescent; c. 1760–70.

26. Large jug of round-necked form, body moulded with overlapping cabbage leaves, painted in onglaze colours with a water scene, bird on a tree and flower sprays—in the manner of the two Corporation of Worcester jugs. Also, a fragment of a waster (level 5) exactly matching the shape of the rim and clearly showing its form. Height, 10½ inches; c. 1755–58.

27. Large jug with mask spout and body moulded with overlapping cabbage leaves, decorated in onglaze colours with an elaborate landscape scene broken in the front by a rare armorial. The arms are those of Brodribb with Berrowe in pretence. There are sprays of 'Meissner blumen' around the neck. Height, $10\frac{1}{2}$ inches; c. 1760.

Colour Plate II. A mask jug with embossed cabbage leaf
body, yellow ground, circular reserves defined by pink scrolls
containing purple printed groups of 'milkmaid' and 'rural
lovers' coloured in, and painted yellow sprays and borders
on ground. Height, 9 inches; c. 1760—65.

28. Teapot and cover: barrel-shaped pot with flat cover and flower knob, embossed with flowers and willow trees and painted in underglaze-blue with floral sprays. Shown with two biscuit wasters (level 5) of the cover and spout, the spout waster showing a typical arrangement of the straining holes. Height, $4\frac{1}{2}$ inches; mark: painter's marks under foot and cover; c. 1758–65.

29. Vase, oviform, painted in onglaze colours with flowers, insects, birds in flight, and a curious curved-beaked bird on a tree. Shown with a matching biscuit waster from pit 4. Height, $6\frac{5}{8}$ inches; c. 1755–60.

30. Round dish of the 'Blind Earl' pattern, painted in naturalistic onglaze colours and with a gold edge, with a biscuit waster (level 4) of exactly matching shape which clearly shows the magnificent moulding of the leaves and the hand-modelled and applied buds. Diameter, $6\frac{1}{5}$ inches; c. 1760–65, but the pattern continues well after this date (Page 50).

31. Finger-bowl and stand, printed in primitive style in onglaze black with birds swimming and flying, a traced line at the edge. Diameter of bowl, 4 inches; height, $3\frac{1}{2}$ inches. Diameter of stand, $6\frac{1}{2}$ inches; c. 1755–1760 (Page 76).

32. Two-handled sauce-boat with lobed lips at each end, the moulded body modelled with leaves, and a multi-petalled leaf around the bottom junction of the handle. These boats of early Worcester shape could be decorated in various ways. This one is printed with onglaze smoky primitive prints of battleships which are tinted-in, the modelled leaves and lobes coloured with bright enamels, the panel at the top of the boat with simple floral sprays. Sometimes the handles have knobs in the form of a monkey's head. Length, $7\frac{1}{2}$ inches; c. 1754–58.

33. Large jug with mas
spout, the body forme
of overlapping cabbag
leaves, printed in onglaz
black and coloured over i
enamels with three scene
engraved by Hancock
'Mayday', after Franci
Hayman—the scene show
in the illustration; and o
either side of it 'rura
lovers', after Gainsborough
and 'milking scene', afte
Luke Sullivan. Height, 9
inches; c. 1760.

35. Tureen in the shap
of a cauliflower, coloure
naturalistically in enamels
decorated with coloured-i
onglaze prints of butter
flies. Derived from Chelse
shapes. Height, 4½ inches
length, 4 inches; c. 1760
1765 (Page 42).

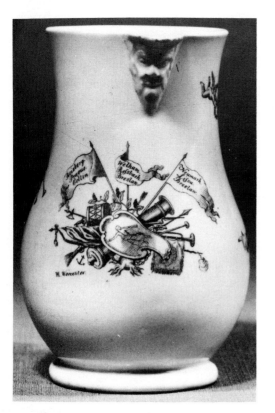

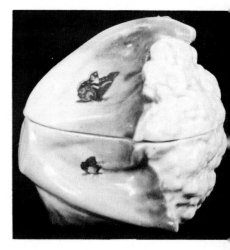

34. Mask jug, plain pear-shaped body
printed in onglaze black with militar
trophies of Frederick the Great, with name
of victories on flags, monogram 'RH' an
anchor. On either side of this are prints c
'fame' blowing a trumpet, and the King c
Prussia, with date '1757'. Height, 5¾ inches
c. 1757–60 (Page 40).

36. A tissue 'pull' taken from an original eighteenth-century copperplate engraved with the 'draw-well' scene. This pull, printed in black ceramic colour, shows the scene in reversed image, which is corrected when the tissue is pressed upon the object to be printed, as seen in Plate 37. The high quality of the engraving is typical of Worcester work.

37. Large straight-sided mug with flat strap handle, very finely transfer-printed in onglaze black with the 'draw-well' scene from the copper-plate of which a pull is shown in Plate 36. Notice how well the print now fits the curving shape of the mug. Height, 5 inches; c. 1760–65 (Page 41).

38. Punch bowl, onglaze black, printed outside with a continuous hunting scene, inside with floral sprays and a hunting scene in the centre. On the right is shown an unglazed waster (level 5) of a bowl of exactly the same size, which shows the typical chamfered edge. Diameter, $9\frac{2}{5}$ inches; c. 1760–65.

39. · Vase and cover, pear-shaped, printed in onglaze black with scenes of classical ruins and sprays of flowers. Height, 13 inches; c. 1760–70.

40. Dish, lobed and pointed sides, printed in onglaze black with a classical scene and a very elaborate border suggestive of the 'willow pattern' underglaze borders. Length, 9½ inches; c. 1770–1780.

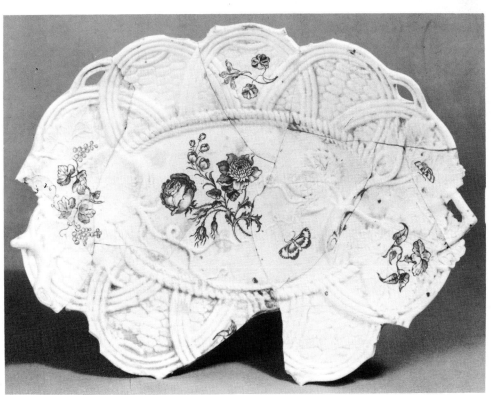

41. Unglazed waster (pit 4): large dish of oval shape, moulded with arcaded basketwork, the ends moulded with vine leaves and stalks, the tendrils spreading over the centre. Length, 11¾ inches; mark: printed hatched crescent with inner line; c. 1760–65.

42. Mask jug, body formed of moulded overlapping cabbage leaves, printed in underglaze-blue with sprays of flowers, including carnation. Shown also is an exactly matching unglazed waster (level 5) which clearly shows the form of the Worcester mask. Height, $7\frac{1}{4}$ inches; mark: under finished piece, a hatched crescent; c. 1770 (Page 37).

43. Large bell-shaped tankard with ribbed strap handle, rim showing typical downward-chamfered edge on the outside, decorated with extremely well controlled underglaze transfer prints of flower sprays and butterflies. Shown with a glazed waster (level 5) of identical shape, with initials 'P. W.' and date '1764' surrounded by a rococo scrolled border, incised through the glaze before firing. This may well have been an apprentice's piece. Height, 6 inches; c. 1765–70 (Page 79).

44. Very rare chamber pot, transfer-printed in underglaze-blue with sprays of flowers and fruit, painted cell border around the rim and flower spray on the handle. Also shown is a waster fragment (level 5) of the exactly matching handle. Diameter, 6⅝ inches; c. 1765–70 (Page 72).

45. Large dish of cabbage-leaf shape, with modelled veins, printed in underglaze-blue with sprays of flowers, fruit and butterflies. Shown with it is an unglazed waster (level 4) of identical shape and with a print from the same copper as the section of the complete leaf dish at the bottom of the photograph. Length, 13 inches; mark: hatched crescent; c. 1765–70.

46. Large two-handled vase of similar shape to the handled vase shown in Colour Plate V. During its hardening-on firing, the rim and handles were broken; but the vessel was glazed and fired. Decorated in underglaze-blue with printed flower sprays, fruit and butterflies and with a painted cell border around the neck. An unglazed waster (level 3) of exactly matching shape and similar prints clearly shows the modelling of the elaborately rococo scrolled handle. Height of vase to damaged glazed-over rim, 12 inches; c. 1765–70 (Page 41).

47. Salad bowl similar in basic outline to those shown in Plate 95 but having a much simpler moulded interior with three scallop shells and a central moulded panel. Decorated inside and outside with underglaze-blue printed floral and fruit sprays, intermediate in style between the decoration in Plates 45 and 48. Matching wasters were found in pits 3, 2 and 1, but the same shape was also made at the Caughley and Lowestoft factories. Diameter, $9\frac{3}{4}$ inches; mark: hatched crescent with central dividing line; c. 1765.

48. Large dish with flat base and wide-necked edge, printed in underglaze-blue in the centre with a magnificent 'blue sprays' group that
developed from the floral sprays shown in Plate 46. Printed butterflies
and sprays surround the main centre group and the whole is surrounded
by an elaborate painted border (number 18). The superb quality of potting,
painting and printing of this dish is typical of the enormous quantity of
such ware made in the overlapping years of the Dr. Wall and Davis/Flight
periods. Length, 12 inches; c. 1770–80 – pit 4 et seq.

49. A round bowl
and cover, the knob
in the form of a
cow lying down,
the cover with a
rounded hole for
a ladle, probably to
hold some form of
butter sauce. Printed
in underglaze-blue
with floral sprays
and butterflies of
early form, and with
a painted border
similar to that on
the 'blue sprays'
print. Diameter of
bowl, 8 inches;
mark: printed
hatched crescent;
c. 1760–68
(Page 76).

50. Vase, with swelling base and a bulbous ridge leading to a tall, wide everted rim, decorated with the 'Queen Charlotte' pattern—sometimes called the 'catherine wheel' or 'whorl' pattern—of alternating spirals of underglaze-blue and on-glaze reds and gold, the layout of which is shown very clearly in the exactly matching hardened-on waster (pit 4). Height, $5\frac{7}{10}$ inches; mark: a fretted square in underglaze-blue, on both waster and finished piece; c. 1760–1770.

52. Cup and saucer, painted in onglaze lavender with an Oriental-type scene. Also, an unglazed waster (level 5) of a matching handle and cup-shape. c. 1760–70.

51 (*opposite*). Bell-shaped tankard, a pale yellow ground reserving two panels in which are painted landscape scenes in a pink/puce monochrome. On the yellow ground are painted Japanese-style flowers in enamels.
Height, $4\frac{5}{8}$ inches; c. 1760–65.

53.   Large coffee pot and cover with vertical flutes, in onglaze enamels
in the Kakiemon style. The pattern is known as the 'partridge' or 'quail'.
The border is a typical one seen on Kakiemon patterns, of floral red and
gold. Height, 9¾ inches; c. 1758–65.

54. Coffee pot and cover of 'feather' moulded form, deriving from just
before 1760, usually found decorated in underglaze-blue with border
number 1. This pot, however, is painted entirely in onglaze colours,
from an Oriental original, with a scene showing Pu-Tai, the corpulent
Chinese monk, with scattered flowers on the ground. Height, $8\frac{1}{4}$ inches;
c. 1758–65.

55. Large leaf dish decorated entirely in onglaze enamels with a scene often called 'the magician', it appearing as if the Chinese man has conjured a vase of flowers on the table in front of the watching ladies. The scene lies cleverly across the veins of the leaf. Length, $8\frac{1}{4}$ inches; c. 1760–70.

Colour Plate III. Patterns from left. Plates, "Kylin" (later used by Chamberlain as his pattern 75 and called "Dragon in Compartments"; "Marchioness of Huntley"; "Bishop Sumber"; Cups and saucers, "Joshua Reynolds" with Ho Ho bird; "Duchess of Kent" with blue ground; "Kempthorne". Dishes, "Earl Manvers; Lord Henry Thynne"; Knife and fork "Archbishop Cobbe. It should not be assumed that everything of similar pattern came from a particular person's service, as many of these were standard patterns. Great confusion exists among collectors between the "Kylin" and "Sumner" pattern, although the "Sumner" pattern has a Kylin fighting a Ho Ho bird and the "Kylin" pattern has creatures that are not really Kylins.

56. Jug with mask lip, the body moulded with overlapping cabbage leaves, painted in onglaze enamels in the style of Chinese 'mandarin'. This typical version shows two ladies and a child by a table in a garden landscape, with panels and borders elaborate diaper similar to cell border. Note the fine, strong handle. Height, 8 inches; c. 1760–70.

57. Tall cream jug or 'Chelsea ewer' with oblique flutes and embossed leaf ornament at the base. Painted in onglaze colours and gilding in the Oriental style, with turquoise scroll border inside the rim and a large spray encircled with a gold wreath on the front, small sprays each side. An exactly matching biscuit waster from the site (level 4) clearly shows the form of the handle, which also occurs on near-matching Caughley examples. Height, 3¾ inches; c. 1770–75.

58. Dessert plate, painted with onglaze enamels in brilliant colours in the Oriental style, the pattern beautifully positioned with sensitive balance Diameter, 9 inches; c. 1765–70.

59. Tea bowl and saucer of so-called 'pencilled' decoration, which is done not with a pencil but with fine brush-work, almost giving the appearance of onglaze printing. The scene is in the 'Jesuit' style. c. 1760–65.

60. Tea bowl and saucer decorated with the 'fan' pattern, the fans composed of alternating underglaze-blue and onglaze red and green panels, divided by three underglaze-blue mons, overlaid with delicate gilding. The centre panel is outlined by a border in underglaze-blue reserving white flower sprays, seen in a number of Oriental-type patterns of this period. Diameter of bowl, $2\frac{9}{10}$ inches; mark: simulated Chinese mark, like the one shown in Plate 1; c. 1760–70.

61.　Coffee cup and saucer of the 'wheatsheaf' pattern, with panels of under-glaze-blue, with gilding reserving circles inside which are chrysanthemums dividing panels of chrysanthemums alternating with wheatsheaves in onglaze colours. A centre chrysanthemum is surrounded by a border of underglaze-blue reserving white flowers and leaves. On the right is a matching waster cup (pit 4) showing the hardened-on underglaze-blue painting. Diameter of cup, $2\frac{4}{5}$ inches; mark: fretted square in underglaze-blue; c. 1760—70.

62.　Magnificent deep dish, the wide rim modelled with four shell corners and elaborate piercing between modelled flowers. The border decorated with tur-quoise and gilding; the inside of the bowl decorated with panels of rouge-de-fer (iron red) reserving circles of chrysanthemums, alternating with panels of Kakiemon-type flowers and prunus, all in onglaze enamels. These fine dishes can have a number of different decorations. Length, $15\frac{1}{2}$ inches; c. 1765—75.

63. Mug of cylindrical shape, pink scale pattern in an irregular-shaped border, with finely painted onglaze scene in the Tenniers style—probably done in Giles' studio. Height, $4\frac{5}{8}$ inches; c. 1770 (Page 50).

64. Round dish, fluted with scalloped edge, pale yellow ground reserving centre in which is a purple print of classical ruins and figures coloured in, flower sprays and ribbon at edge. Width, 10 inches; c. 1760–65.

65. Junket dish painted with sprays of flowers in recessed panels outlined by puce-edged scrolls, continued to form the border around the shaped rim, all reserved on a canary-yellow basket moulded ground. Also, a waster of exactly the same shape (pit 3). Length, $8\frac{7}{8}$ inches; c. 1760–65.

66. Coffee pot and cover, yellow ground reserving scroll-shaped panels containing onglaze flower sprays in a sophisticated style, detached flower sprays on ground. Height, 6 inches; c. 1760–68.

67. Two mustard pots. The dry-mustard pot, on the left, is painted in enamels with Oriental figures and flowers. The wet-mustard pot, on the right, has onglaze paintings of European-type flowers and a solid handle similar to the pierced form in Plate 74. The flower knob on the wet-mustard pot is not original. Heights, $4\frac{1}{2}$ and $3\frac{1}{2}$ inches; left, c. 1755–58, right, c. 1770.

68. Fine large mask jug, painted in onglaze colours with gilding, green ground leaving a waved bordering at the rim and reserving gold-edged panels containing exotic birds, foliage and landscape, and smaller panels containing birds in flight. Note that the gilding is clear of the green ground, on which it could not be placed. Height, 8¼ inches; c. 1765 (Page 48).

69. Large dish of oval shape, twelve-sided, painted in onglaze colours with gilding. Apple green and scroll-edged border, from which depend festoons of fruit and red-berried foliage to a green and red border at centre surrounding green flower and gilt foliage. Length, $11\frac{1}{2}$ inches; c. 1760–65.

70. Cake plate of saucer-dish shape. A strong claret or ruby ground reserving a centre painted in brilliant onglaze enamels with birds on fruit sprays by the 'sliced fruit' painter, with elaborate broad-leaved chased gilding. The whole effect is typical of Giles' decoration. Diameter, 7 inches; c. 1768–70 (Page 50).

71.   Round dish with wavy ribbed flutes and a scrolled panel, painted in
brilliant onglaze enamels with fabulous birds, fruit and butterflies, typical
of the style of Giles' decorators. Diameter, $10\frac{1}{4}$ inches; c. 1765–70
(Page 50).

72. Bowl, or slop basin, with powdered underglaze-blue ground reserving fan and circular reserves in which are painted sprays of flowers, in onglaze enamels and outlined with gilding, in the European style. On the right is an unglazed waster (pit 4) of exactly the same shape, size and underglaze decoration, clearly showing the typical Worcester chamfered rim on the outside. Diameter, 6 inches; height, 3 inches; c. 1760–70.

73. Plate, scalloped edge of twenty-four lobes, gros-blue ground surrounding circular centre containing fabulous birds in landscape painted in onglaze enamels. Shown with an exactly matching glazed waster (pit 1). Diameter, $7\frac{3}{4}$ inches; marks: on both pieces, fretted squares; c. 1768–72.

74. Caudle or chocolate cup, cover and stand, decorated in underglaze scale blue reserving vase- and mirror-shaped panels in which are painted fabulous birds, flowers and insects in onglaze enamels. The simple and reticent Worcester gilding should be compared with that in Plate 80. Shown on the right is an unglazed waster (pit 1), of identical shape and underglaze decoration, which clearly shows the scales and outlining of the reserve panels. This form of handle may be either pierced or solid, and chocolate and caudle cups may have only one. Diameter of cup, $3\frac{3}{4}$ inches; mark: fretted square; c. 1775.

75. Cup and saucer decorated with underglaze scale blue reserving vase- and mirror-shaped reserves in which are painted fabulous birds, flowers and insects in onglaze enamels, with simple gilding around the panels in Worcester style. On the right is shown an unglazed waster (pit 1), of exactly the same size and underglaze decoration, which clearly shows the scaling and the characteristic handle shape. Diameter of cup, $3\frac{1}{4}$ inches; mark: fretted square in underglaze-blue, under all three pieces; c. 1775.

76. Teapoy of ovoid shape, decorated with underglaze scale blue, with large reserved panels very finely painted in onglaze enamels with fabulous birds in a landscape scene. Gilding around the panels and at neck and foot. The cover, with a flower finial, is an unglazed waster (pit 1), which repeats on its rim the floral border on the neck of the teapoy. Height to top of neck, $5\frac{1}{4}$ inches; mark: fretted square; c. 1775.

77. Large round punch bowl (somewhat distorted), painted in under-glaze-blue and onglaze colours with gilding; blue ground on outside reserving three oval panels containing garlands of coloured flowers; inside, twelve small blue medallions gilded with flowers, and a spray of coloured flowers. Diameter, 11 inches; mark: open crescent in under-glaze-blue; c. 1765–70.

78. Bough pot, or crocus pot, lobed front and side, with a flat back leading up to a rococo scrolled top through which are two circular holes for affixing the pot to the wall. The inside cover is pierced with one large hole and many small holes. Painted in underglaze scale blue and onglaze colours with gilding. Width, $8\frac{3}{4}$ inches; mark: fretted square in underglaze-blue; c. 1760–70.

79. One of a pair of vases and covers of hexagonal snape, underglaze scale blue ground reserving large panels in which are painted elaborate Chinoiserie figures. Smaller panels contain birds and insects. Height, 11½ inches; mark: a fretted square; c. 1775.

80.   Plate of the so-called 'Lady Mary Wortley Montague' pattern; an underglaze scale blue ground reserving three panels in which are onglaze scenes of birds and foliage, outlined with elaborate gilding incorporating broad leaves in the style of the London decorators. Decorated by Giles. Diameter, $8\frac{3}{4}$ inches; mark: a fretted square; c. 1768–70 (Page 50).

81.   Two mugs decorated with underglaze scale blue and onglaze decoration. The mug on the left is a late nineteenth century fake. Notice the very perfect, printed look of the scales on the fake—the stiffer, more careful painting; the brassier appearance of the gilding, and the whiter hard-paste body. Height of genuine piece on the right, 5 inches; mark: fretted square on genuine mug c. 1770 and painted crescent on the fake (Page 89).

Colour Plate IV. A large tureen and cover with oval gadroon edge, shell handles and flower-bud knob, magnificently painted onglaze with large groups of fruit, fungi etc., between small blue and gold panels containing butterflies; green and gold hatching at edge. This splendid design is known as the 'Duke of Gloucester' pattern as it is believed that a service of this design was made for William Henry, Duke of Gloucester, 1743–1805. Length, 10½ inches; mark: a large gold crescent; c. 1768–74 (Page 50).

Colour Plate V. Two vases underglaze-blue ground, the one on the right painted by Donaldson with 'Leda and the Swan', after Boucher; the one on the left painted by O'Neale with 'Leopards and Lions' (on the other side of this vase is 'Mars, Venus and Cupid'). Also see Plate 83. Heights, 11¼ and 12½ inches; marks: fretted squares in underglaze-blue; c. 1768—1770 (Page 53).

82. Vase, goblet-shaped, with pierced rim, painted in underglaze scale blue reserving eight scroll-edged panels—seven containing flowers and one containing cupids. Finely gilded. Although unsigned, almost certainly the work of John Donaldson. Height, 7 inches; c. 1770 (Page 53).

83. Garniture of three vases of baluster shape with scroll handles. Blue ground reserving two heart-shaped panels containing figure groups painted by John Donaldson (signed 'J D' in monogram), after subjects by Boucher: 'Europa and the Bull', 'The Birth of Bacchus' and 'Leda and the Swan'. The panels on the other side of the vases contain flower groups with fountain and vases. The right-hand vase is also shown in Colour Plate V. Heights, 18 and $12\frac{1}{2}$ inches; marks: fretted squares in underglaze-blue; c. 1768–70 (Page 53).

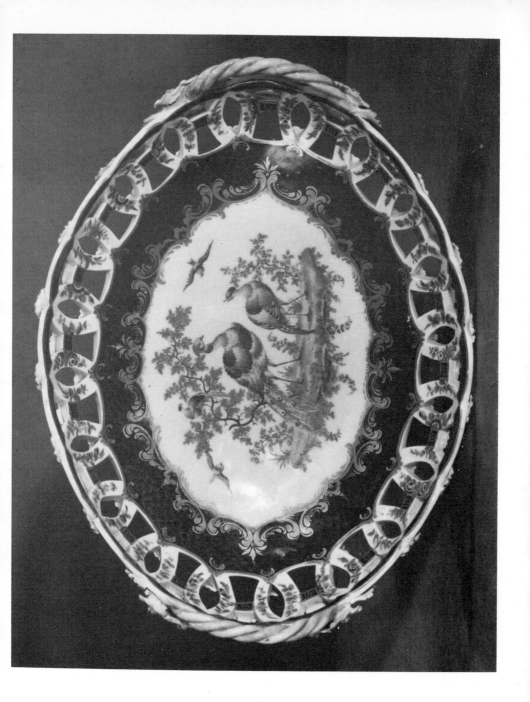

84. Pierced oval dessert basket dish with moulded and applied leaves on the outside. Twisted-rope handles, underglaze scale blue decoration reserving a central panel containing fabulous birds in a landscape in onglaze enamels, surrounded by gilding. Length, 11 inches; mark: underglaze script 'W'; c. 1768–76.

85. Tea bowl of prunus-root' pattern and saucer of 'prunus fence' pattern painted in underglaze-blue. On each side of the finished tea bowl is an unglazed waster (pit 1) placed so as to show the complete sequence of the pattern around the bowl. This scene was painted by a number of different painters and runs from about 1755 to about 1770. The long life of the pattern is illustrated by the saucer of about 1755 and the waster bowls of about 1770. Mark: under the saucer, a painter's mark like a key; under each waster tea bowl, a painted open crescent.

86. Five wasters from the site, of unusual patterns or of ones that are not in the Perrins Museum Collection. The saucer on the left is of a well-known Chinese type, but the main underglaze scene is intended for finishing off with onglaze enamels. Next to it is a sparrow-beak milk jug painted underglaze with a 'landslip' pattern. On the right, a bowl painted with a 'bird in a ring' pattern; flowers in a strange three-legged pot and a landscape with 'billboard' type rocks complete the scene. Below, left, is a Chinese-figure scene; and on the right, the inside pattern on a glazed sauce-boat rim fragment—of a type which is often ascribed to Derby.

87. Biscuit waster (levels 5 and 4) of similar moulded 'chrysanthemum' type pattern to the saucer shown in Plate 88. Normally, this is finished off with border number 3 and, inside the bowl, a painted chrysanthemum. Notice the very fine modelling—the thinnest parts of the bowl providing a beautiful effect when held up to the light—and the large fire crack that obviously led to the wastage of the bowl. Diameter, $2\frac{3}{4}$ inches; c. 1760–70 (Page 57).

88. Saucer, most of the interior moulded with leaves and flowers of chrysanthemum type, a narrow border of pattern number 3 (found only on this moulded pattern and on the straight reeded flute) and a large, finely painted chrysanthemum in the centre. Shown on the saucer is a fragment of an unglazed waster (level 5) of exactly matching shape and pattern, probably by the same painter. On some forms, the moulded pattern can cover the whole saucer. Mark: open painted crescent; c. 1758–70.

89. A group of knife-and-fork-handle and spoon shapes from the site—
except for the finished salt spoon, shown with a matching waster bowl.
The handles represent pistol-grip and round types, and one modelled with
flowers and leaves. The spoon with a frilled end is very rare. The finished
spoon, decorated underglaze, is $3\frac{9}{10}$ inches long. Wasters from various
levels, c. 1760–66.

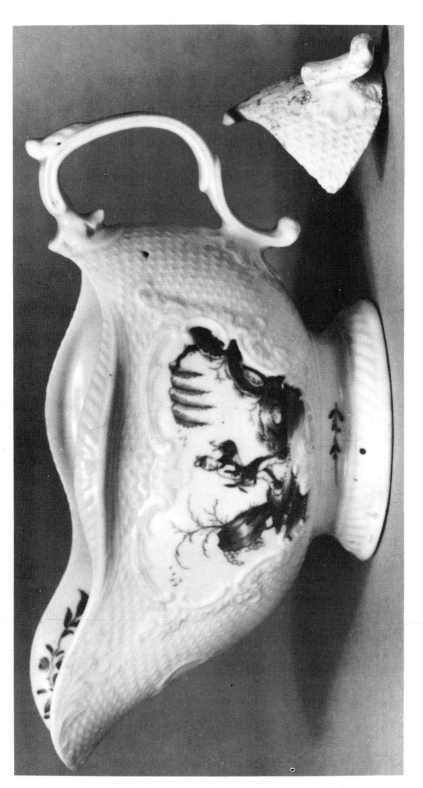

90. Sauce-boat, modelled with basketwork and rococo panels in which are painted landscape scenes with a man holding some form of plant; a fishing scene on the other side; floral spray inside the lip in underglaze-blue. On the right is shown a waster (level 4) of exactly matching shape which shows the shell pattern around the lower junction of the handle. Length, 8 inches; mark: open painted crescent; c. 1756–65.

91. Teapot and cover, painted in underglaze-blue with the 'cannonball' scene—a landscape embodying a group of three round blobs. On the left is shown a waster fragment (level 4) of the same shape and pattern; and on the right is a fragment of a bowl from the same level which clearly shows the typical cross-shading and the detail of the 'pylons' in the distance. Height of pot, $5\frac{1}{2}$ inches; mark: painted crescent, initials 'W. M.' and date '1766' with a scrolled border, under the base. (Although the pot is dated 1766, the pattern's life-span was c. 1756–75) (Page 55).

92. Egg-cup, painted with floral sprays and diaper border in underglaze-blue. On the right is a waster of similar shape; and on the left is a waster of a type having modelled sprays of flowers on the body and foot. Both wasters are from level 5. Diameter of finished egg-cup, $2\frac{3}{4}$ inches; mark: open painted crescent; c. 1758–65 (Page 74).

93. Three trays from an hors-d'œuvres set, with painted floral sprays and birds, the tray on the right being an unglazed waster (pit 4) as is also the portion of the star-shaped centrepiece around which six trays were meant to fit. Length of centrepiece, $3\frac{1}{2}$ inches; length of trays, 3 inches; mark: on flat bases of trays, an open painted crescent; c. 1760–70 (Page 30).

94. Coffee cup and saucer, painted in underglaze-blue with 'two quails' pattern, shown with a fragment of a glazed waster bowl (level 3) of the same pattern but of a later date. Mark: painted open crescents; cup and saucer, c. 1765–70, but the pattern continues (Page 58).

95. Three different forms of salad or junket dishes, all wasters (pit 1), decorated in underglaze-blue with different forms of floral and fruit sprays and either floral or cell borders in the panels around the rim. Diameter, $9\frac{2}{5}$ inches; mark on centre dish: a painted open crescent; c. 1760–70.

96. Mug, bell-shaped, painted in underglaze-blue with figure scene in Chinese style. The other side of the mug shows a seated lady. Height, $5\frac{3}{4}$ inches; mark: open painted crescent; c. 1768–75.

97. Chamber candlestick, shell modelled edge, candle-holder placed a little off centre with a pierced hole through its base, a mask joining the handle to the dish. Painted underglaze with sprays of flowers in late style. Also, an unglazed waster (pit 1) of exactly matching form clearly showing the modelling of the mask. The basic shape was also made at Caughley. Diameter, $5\frac{1}{10}$ inches; mark: open painted crescent; c. 1765–70.

98. Teapot and cover, decorated in underglaze-blue with powdered ground reserving fan-shaped and circular panels containing scenes in the Chinese style derived from delft. Height, $5\frac{1}{2}$ inches; mark: open crescent and fretted square; c. 1760–65.

99.   Sauce-boat of pleasing moulded shape, painted underglaze with large floral sprays of late type in the two main panels, with small sprays and a painted cell border. Shown also is a biscuit waster (level 4, and pits 2 and 1) of exactly the same form. This basic shape was also made at Caughley. Length, 6¾ inches; mark: open painted crescent; c. 1768–80.

100.   Plate with scalloped edge of typical Worcester shape, painted underglaze with Chinese mythological objects known as the 'hundred antiques'. Diameter, 8½ inches; mark: imitation Chinese symbol; c. 1765.

101.   Dessert dish, painted different tones of underglaze-blue with what is probably a direct copy of a Chinese original. Length, 9¾ inches; mark: an imitation Chinese symbol in underglaze-blue; c. 1770–75.

102.   Bowl, painted underglaze with a 'candle fence and gate' pattern, the gate posts having candle-like knobs; a spindly willow tree and landscape; herringbone border number 21, only found on this pattern. A variant has the 'candle fence' with a landslip on the reverse. On the left is a matching waster (pit 4) but by a different hand. Diameter, 6 inches; mark: painted open crescent; c. 1760–70.

103. Mug of cylindrical shape, painted in underglaze-blue with the 'Chinese gardener' pattern: two Chinese, and a table with a flower in a vase; one of the Chinese in the act of planting or pulling up a plant in a steeply sloping garden. On the right, a matching waster (pit 1; also found in pit 2), but painted by a different hand, which shows the typical chamfered rim. Height, $5\frac{3}{4}$ inches; mark: open painted crescent; c. 1768–1775.

Colour Plate VI. Rare Worcester figures of the Dr. Wall Period; a pair of a Turk and his companion, height 5 inches; a group of Canaries on apple blossom, height 6½ inches; and a pair of Gardener, and his companion, the Gardener, height 10½ inches set up as a candlestick with bocage; his companion, height 6¼ inches, left plain.

104. Tea bowl and saucer, twenty-four vertical flutes ending in points, the saucer deep with countersunk foot-rim, painted underglaze with a flowering rock and a long-tailed bird, elaborate border number 17, which is mainly found on this pattern. On the right is an unglazed waster (pit 1) of a saucer one size larger than the finished one. Note the fine quality of this late period painting. Mark: open painted crescent; c. 1768–80.

105. Cream jug of barrel shape, embossed scrolls and ridged bands top and bottom, painted underglaze with sprays and a cell border at rim. On the right is an unglazed waster (pit 1) of matching shape, with painted cell borders at rim and foot, clearly showing the quality of the moulding. Height, $2\frac{3}{4}$ inches; mark: open painted crescent; c. 1765–70.

106. Cup and saucer with straight flutes, painted underglaze with the 'Meissen Onion' or 'Immortelle' pattern. Shown with an exactly matching waster (level 4) of a saucer. Quite often, the blue runs very heavily down the flutes—especially on tea bowls. From the Rous Lench Collection; c. 1765–75.

107. Two tea bowls and saucers, painted in underglaze-blue with the 'Mansfield' pattern. The tea bowl and saucer on the left are finished pieces; the ones on the right are unglazed wasters (pit 1). Although of identical pattern, the wasters are not painted by the same hand; differences in technique may be clearly observed and should be looked for in all examples of this and the many other common patterns. Diameter of finished bowl, $2\frac{7}{10}$ inches; marks: open painted crescents; c. 1765–75 (Page 58).

108. Sugar bowl and cover, the cover with a flower knob, painted in underglaze-blue with floral sprays and border number 2—the only pattern with which this border is associated. The pattern is called 'Mansfield', under which name it is produced by the Worcester Royal Porcelain Company today. Shown with two wasters (level 4). Height, $5\frac{1}{2}$ inches; mark: open painted crescent; c. 1770, but the pattern runs from about 1760 to 1775.

109. Pickle dish of leaf shape, painted in underglaze-blue with floral sprays and edging. The left-hand piece is a waster (levels 4 and 2) of exactly matching shape; it is turned over to show the delicate modelling of the veins underneath. Similar leaves were made at several other factories but the modelling of the waster can be taken as positive proof of Worcester origin. Length, $3\frac{1}{4}$ inches; mark: painted open crescent; c. 1768–80.

110. Asparagus butter-boat, shaped in plan like a leaf, three three-leafed-clover-like leaves for the feet, painted underglaze with leaf spray and cell border. Also, an unglazed waster (level 5) of same shape turned over to show the base. This shape was made at several factories, including Caughley. Length, $3\frac{1}{4}$ inches; mark: painted open crescent; c. 1760–70.

111. Two cream-boats or pickle dishes of overlapping-leaf shape. The one on the right is a biscuit waster (level 4); the rim is of wavy shape; the handle has a curved, flattened thumb-rest, and continues under and through the base of the vessel. The left-hand boat is decorated under-glaze with late floral sprays. Height, $1\frac{1}{4}$ inches; length, $3\frac{1}{2}$ inches; c. 1770–75.

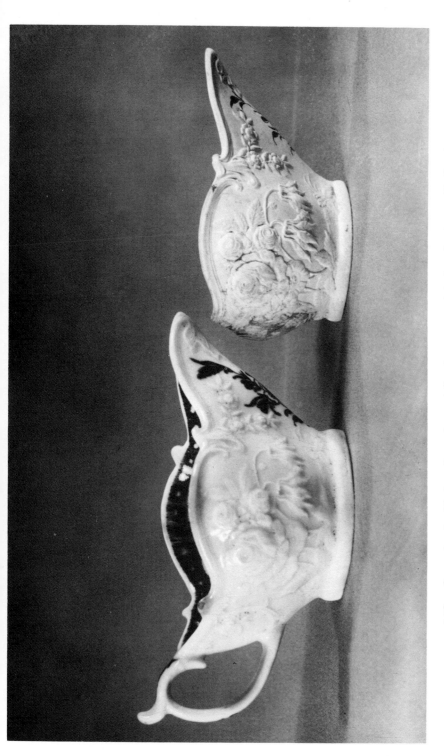

112. Sauce-boat with heavily embossed floral sprays, painted underglaze with floral spray under the lip and a cell border inside. On the right is an unglazed waster (pit 1) of exactly matching form which clearly shows the modelling. Length, 7 inches; mark: open painted crescent; c. 1765–75.

113. Mug, bell-shaped, painted in onglaze enamels and gilding; with the arms and crest of Thomson on the front, surrounded by a ruined-colonnade scene in lilac. Height, $3\frac{3}{8}$ inches; c. 1758–60.

114.   Tureen in the form of a partridge sitting on its nest, the upper part lifting off to form the cover, naturalistically painted in onglaze colours. For a long time, these were thought to be Chelsea. But they are mentioned in the price list quoted in Chapter 1; and the fragment of the tail feather shown, from level 4, exactly matches the corresponding section of the complete tureen. Two sizes of partridge are mentioned. This one is $7\frac{1}{2}$ inches long and 5 inches wide; c. 1757–70. (Page 50).

115. Teapot and cover, and milk jug with entwined handle, fluted spout to the teapot, painted in onglaze colours with birds perched on branches, bird in flight and sprays of flowers, an irregular yellow diapered border and slight gilding—very much in the Meissen style. Also shown, an exactly matching biscuit waster handle (pit 3). Decoration by Giles. Height of teapot, $6\frac{1}{2}$ inches; height of jug, $4\frac{1}{2}$ inches; mark: crossed swords, and numeral '9' in underglaze-blue: c. 1762–70.

116. Oval tray of 'Blind Earl' moulded shape, painted in onglaze colours with sprays of flowers, a purple line at the edge. Also, an unglazed waster (pit 2) exactly the same. Length, 6 inches; c. 1760–70.

117. Covered sucrier and stand with moulded basket-weave border and groups of double wavy lines reserving panels in which are painted onglaze sprays of flowers. Biscuit fragment (level 4, also pits 2 and 1) is of the stand and shows the inner ring into which the bowl fits. Overall height, $4\frac{1}{2}$ inches; diameter of bowl rim, $5\frac{7}{10}$ inches; diameter of stand, $6\frac{1}{2}$ inches; mark: a blue cross, under bowl and stand; c. 1765–75.

118. Tureen and cover, the knob in the form of an artichoke and leaves, the rims with moulded basket-work, the base with two shell-like handles. Decorated onglaze with the fable of the fox and the grapes in the style of O'Neale, and with gilt dentil border. The basic shape was also made at Caughley. Length across handles, $9\frac{1}{2}$ inches. c. 1770–75.

119. Plate, embossed basket-work-pattern rim, painted sprays of flowers in onglaze colours with gold edge. Also, matching fragment from pit 1. Diameter, $9\frac{1}{2}$ inches; c. 1770–80.

120.   Large ornamental vase and cover, globular, with foot, pierced
shoulder and cover, modelled grapes as knob. Painted sprays of flowers
in 'dry' blue onglaze colour with gilding. Height, $17\frac{1}{2}$ inches; c. 1770–78
(Page 54).

121. Large oval dish with fluted sides, of the 'Lord Henry Thynne' pattern, with a landscape scene after the style of O'Neale in onglaze enamels and gilding. Probably London decorated. This is decorated in a distinctive style after a simple decoration had been removed by acid, the new decoration being contemporary. Length, 11½ inches; c. 1770–75.

122.   Oval chestnut tureen and cover with moulded body, the cover with pierced panels, with applied twig handles and flowers painted in under-glaze-blue, shown with an unglazed waster stand (pit 3) of similar form, very finely painted with a fence, flowering rocks with a bird, surrounded by cell border. An identical complete stand is shown in Watney's *English Blue and White Porcelain of the Eighteenth Century*, Plate 57B, the foot-ring of the basket of which has an impressed 'T°' mark. Length of stand, 10 inches; mark: open printed crescent; c. 1768–75.

123.   Sweetmeat stand formed of four large shells, one cup-like sur-mounting the three scallop-shaped, attached to and supported by many small shells and seaweed. Painted borders and floral sprays in underglaze-blue. Height, $5\frac{1}{2}$ inches; width, $8\frac{1}{2}$ inches; c. 1770 (Page 83).

124. Oval dessert dish modelled with leaves and basket-work, diamond-shaped piercing in the well. Painted borders and tracing on leaves in underglaze-blue. A fragment of a waster (level 4) is placed on the right-hand end of the dish, showing it to exactly match the complete dish. Length, $11\frac{3}{4}$ inches; c. 1770–75.

125. Sugar bowl and cover with straight flutes, the cover having a floral knob. Painted underglaze with sprays of gilly flowers (or 'Chantilly sprig') and insects, and painted rim. On the right is a waster (level 4) of exactly matching shape and decoration which clearly shows the wavy edge at the top of the fluted bowl. Height to rim of bowl, $3\frac{1}{4}$ inches; mark: open painted crescent; c. 1770–80.

126. Tea canister and cover with flat button knob, cylindrical, widening up to the shoulder and vertically ribbed, printed in onglaze black with groups of milkmaids and a man with animals; birds on cover. This scene was also printed in underglaze-blue. Height, 4½ inches; c. 1776–80.

127. Tokens made at a time of shortage of small change, presumably used as wages for the factory employees. The tokens for both one shilling and two shillings, shown with the modern coin for each amount, are printed onglaze and are extremely rare. On the reverse are the moulded letters 'W P C', for Worcester Porcelain Company. c. 1770–80.

128. Teapot and cover, straight flutes, printed in onglaze black with figures and ruins, gilded borders and knob. Height, $6\frac{1}{2}$ inches; c. 1780–85.

Colour Plate VII. A covered basket and stand, of the type referred to as a roast-chestnut basket or tureen, the cover and stand embossed and pierced, and the body embossed with flower and honeycomb diaper; twig handles with applied flowers and leaves; painted in onglaze colours. Height, 6 inches; length, 10½ inches; c. 1768—76.

129. Figure group of Cupid at Vulcan's forge, long ascribed to Longton Hall, shown with a fragment of a model in pitcher from level 3. The model exactly matches the forge part of the finished group, allowing for a reduction of about a sixth in firing. Height of finished group, 6½ inches. Height of model, 4 inches. Probably around 1760–70 in date. Finished group from the collection of Dr. B. Watney.

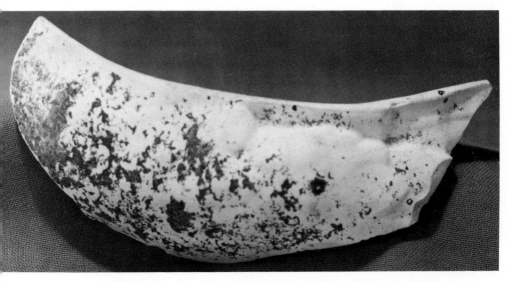

130. Biscuit waster (level 3) of the rim of the base of a tureen, modelled with the tail feathers of a bird—possibly a swan, or some such bird. Length of waster, 8 inches; probable length of rim, 12 inches. Not later than about 1780 (Page 51).

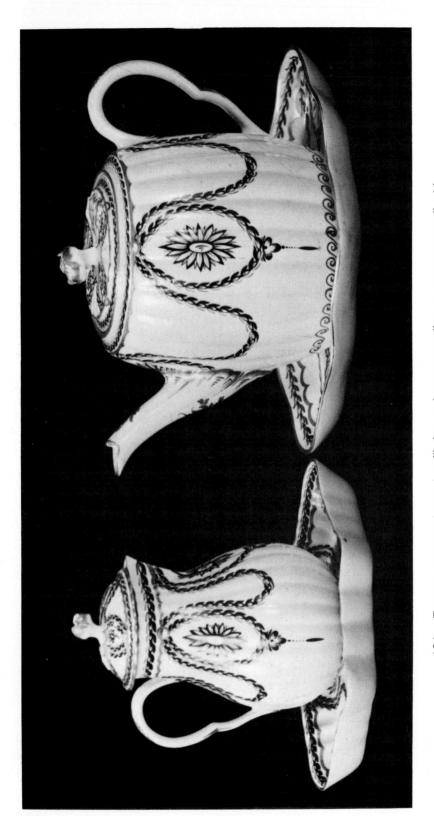

131. Teapot, cover and stand, milk jug and cover standing on spoon tray, all with straight fluting, handles of ear shape, decorated onglaze with black-husk pattern and gilding. Height of teapot, $5\frac{1}{4}$ inches; Davis/Flight Period, c. 1776–90 (Page 54).

132. Tea bowl printed in underglaze-blue with 'mother and child and a man fishing' pattern, set in a rococo scrolled and diaper border. On the left is an unglazed waster (disturbed levels) printed from the same copper-plate. Diameter, $2\frac{9}{10}$ inches; mark: hatched crescent; c. 1770–80.

133. Large cylindrical mug, printed in underglaze-blue with a Chinoiserie, 'La Pêche'. Height, $5\frac{1}{4}$ inches; diameter, $5\frac{3}{4}$ inches; mark: hatched crescent; c. 1774–80.

134. A saucer of the 'fence' pattern. In front of the saucer are three unglazed wasters (pit 1), from left to right: a coffee cup, a tea bowl and a coffee can arranged to show the complete scene. Heights of the wasters: cup, $2\frac{1}{2}$ inches—bowl, $1\frac{9}{16}$ inches—can, $2\frac{5}{16}$ inches; marks: printed hatched crescents; c. 1765—1785 (Page 62).

135. Bowl, printed underglaze with the 'fisherman' pattern, shown with the considerably distorted foot of an identical sized and decorated bowl (level 3). Diameter, 9 inches; mark: hatched crescent; c. 1776–93 (Page 63).

136. Saucer dish printed underglaze in a pale tone of blue with the 'fisherman' pattern. Shown with wasters (level 3) of four different shapes, all printed from different sized coppers of the same pattern. Diameter, 7 inches; mark: disguised numeral 8; c. 1776–1793.

137. Two tea bowls and saucers of the Davis/Flight Period, shown with wasters (level 3) exactly matching the saucers. Both bowls are printed underglaze, the scene on the left being 'European figures in landscape' and on the right 'two figures in temple landscape'. Marks: hatched crescents on left-hand pieces and disguised numerals on right-hand pieces; c. 1776—93.

138. Two waster tea bowls (level 3), the one on the left unglazed, with a hardened-on print of classical figures in a ruined landscape, and an elaborate border; mark underneath, a disguised numeral 8. The bowl on the right is a fully glazed waster with defects that caused a hole to be smashed in its base, printed underglaze with the 'three flowers' pattern, two underglaze painted lines inside. c. 1776–90.

139. Three milk jugs of the Davis/Flight Period, printed underglaze in a violet-toned blue. The patterns are, left to right, 'temple', 'two figures in temple landscape', and 'bat'. Heights and marks, left to right: $3\frac{2}{5}$ inches, disguised numeral 2; $4\frac{1}{2}$ inches, disguised numeral 8; $3\frac{3}{4}$ inches, disguised numeral 1. c. 1780–90. *From the Geoffrey Godden Collection.*

140. Coffee pot, teapot and covers of the Davis/Flight Period, printed underglaze in a strong violet-toned blue—the coffee pot with the 'bat' pattern and the teapot with the 'fisherman and cormorant'. Shown also is a teapot waster (level 3) of a size larger than the complete one. Coffee pot height, 9 inches; mark: disguised numeral 2. Teapot height, 5 inches; mark: hatched crescent; c. 1776–1793. *From the Geoffrey Godden Collection.*

141. Sugar bowl and cover, with flat button knob, and teapot stand printed underglaze in a strong tone of violet-blue with the 'argument' pattern, shown with a waster (level 3) of exactly the same shape as the teapot stand and printed from the same copper. Diameter of sugar bowl, 4 inches; height of bowl and cover, $5\frac{1}{5}$ inches; mark: disguised numeral 7. Length of stand, $5\frac{9}{10}$ inches; mark: disguised numeral 7; c. 1780–93. *From the Geoffrey Godden Collection* (Page 63).

142. Mug, cylindrical, painted underglaze with the 'royal lily' pattern (also made at other factories), gilding on the borders and a red-brown edge. Also, an unglazed waster (level 3) of a mug rim. Height, $4\frac{3}{8}$ inches; mark: open crescent; Davis/Flight Period, c. 1780–90 (Page 62).

143. Basket with pierced panels and moulded flowers, applied twisted-rope handles, painted inside with the 'royal lily' pattern in underglaze-blue; rim, handles and flower centres painted blue. Basic shape also made at Caughley. Length, $9\frac{1}{2}$ inches; mark: 'Flight', in underglaze-blue script, and a painted open crescent; c. 1783–93 (Page 62).

144. Cup and saucer, spirally fluted, decorated with underglaze-blue diamonds and flowers and gilded leaves. Also a glazed but ungilded waster (level 3) of exactly the same shape and decoration as the saucer. Height of cup, $2\frac{1}{2}$ inches; mark: painted open crescent underglaze; c. 1785–95 (Page 62).

145. Beaker, straight sided, similar decoration to Plate 146. Height, $3\frac{1}{4}$ inches; mark: open crescent; c. 1780–90.

146. Mask jug, body moulded with overlapping cabbage leaves, decorated with underglaze-blue and gold, with vertical blue and gold stripes
broken by gold medallions dividing longitudinal sprays of blue flowers
and gold foliage. Height, 9 inches; marks: open crescent and script
'Flight' in underglaze-blue; c. 1783–90.

147. A group of interesting wasters from the site. From left to right: the top of a straight-sided pot with gadrooned rim, inside ledge and two moulded bands on the outside with false 'mooring ring' handles, probably a pot of flowers; base of an eyebath with knopped foot; base of a small vase; section of a three-legged pierced bowl; below the latter, the base of a vase probably standing on a squared base, the foot with spiral gadroonings; and a group of three glazed buttons, two of them with underglaze-blue and probably intended for onglaze decoration. Similar buttons were found at the Caughley site. Diameter of largest button, 1¼ inches; buttons, level 3, c. 1780–90.

148. A large dish from the magnificent service made for the Duke of Clarence in 1792, painted in monochrome by John Pennington with a different scene of 'Hope and the Anchor' on each piece, the border being finely gilded over underglaze-blue. (The two large tureens from this service are illustrated, separately, by G. A. Godden—one in his *British Pottery and Porcelain, 1780–1850*, 1963, the other in the *Illustrated Encyclopaedia of British Pottery and Porcelain*, 1966.) Length, 19½ inches; mark: 'Flight' in script, a crown above and a small crescent below, all in underglaze-blue (Page 65).

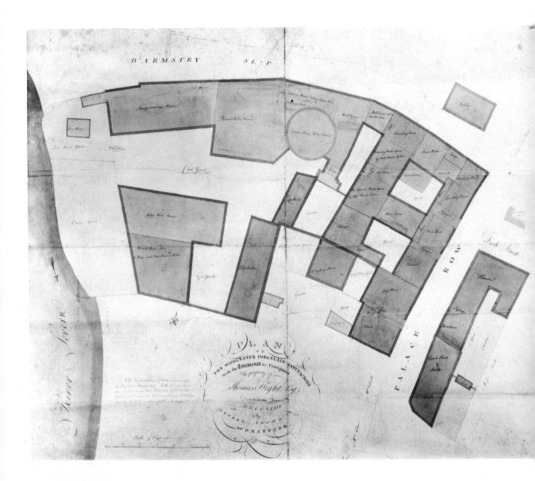

149. Plan of the Worcester Porcelain Manufactory, 1793, drawn by
George Young of Worcester, which shows that the main group of kiln
buildings running up Warmstry Slip to Warmstry House had not changed
very much from the scene shown in Plates 3 and 4. The archaeological
excavation ran from above the arrow showing the flow of the river, across
the 'ember yard'. The plan is the property of the Worcester Corporation,
and shows the property was still noted as being owned by Thomas Flight.
The main changes over the earlier look of the factory are an ember yard
added on and a curving brick wall built out into the river frontage (Page
65).

Colour Plate VIII. A coffee pot and cover, very beautifully painted with sprays of flowers in a puce pink camaieu, some of them in gold scroll cartouche in the Meissen style. Some of the examples of this late form of decoration use the crossed swords mark. Height, 8½ inches; c. 1775–1785.

The Ware

BRISTOL AND BRISTOL/WORCESTER

Apart from the few pieces marked with the embossed word BRISTOL (or, alternatively, BRISTOLL), the figure of the Chinaman, and the sauce- and cream- or butter-boats—which clearly must have been made at Miller & Lund's factory in Bristol—it is obvious from the discoveries at Warmstry House that it is very difficult to ascribe any other early pieces with certainty. So many of the shapes that have always been confidently ascribed to Bristol were found on the site that it is clear that not only were the basic moulds brought up to Worcester at the amalgamation but some of the mouldmakers must have come as well.

There is no other explanation for the fragment shown in Plate 5, which a number of present-day Worcester designers and workmen have confidently declared to be by the same mouldmaker as the complete piece shown in the same photograph. How else can one explain the fragment shown in Plate 2, which is identical to the Bristol marked boat shown next to it? These fragments were found in a level which could be as late as 1758, together with many fragments of similar contemporary silver shapes.

This suggests that a very large number of pieces ascribed to Bristol should strictly be called Worcester, especially if they correspond with fragments found on the site. In fact, I will go further and suggest that all possessors of pieces thought to be from Miller & Lund's factory should have a fresh look at them in the light of the discoveries. It is relevant to note here that according to a document discovered by Dr. B. Watney in the Public Record Office, Benjamin Lund, formerly of Bristol, was in Worcester in February 1753 and described as a 'china maker'—a fact that underlines the continuation of the Bristol influence found on early Worcester porcelain.

Failing an excavation ever becoming possible on the site of Miller & Lund's factory, I would like to suggest that it is much safer to designate only those pieces as Bristol that are marked with the actual embossed word, and all others as Bristol/Worcester or Worcester. I realise that this is going to remove from collections the great majority of pieces ascribed to Bristol, as marked pieces are very rare, but feel it is wrong to ignore the evident fact that the Bristol factory made fewer pieces than has always been thought.

Bristol

The marked Bristol pieces are very interesting as a group. The five in the Perrins Museum, shown together in Plate 2, exhibit most of the characteristics of these rare pieces. The Chinaman is based upon a Chinese figure of Lu Tung-Pin and is particularly interesting in being the only dated Bristol piece; for as well as the word 'Bristol', he carries embossed on his back the date '1750'—the year before the formation of the Worcester Porcelain Company. The figure is a very simple one, from a two-piece mould, covered with a thick glaze which varies somewhat in the seven known examples and covers up most of the obviously very fine modelling lying underneath. One of these figures, in the Victoria and Albert Museum, has the base stained with underglaze manganese, which is much more difficult to handle in firing than cobalt.

The sauce-boats are all fairly long and shallow, with flamboyant curved handles and curled thumb-rests. The cream-boats are more restrained and are of two types: a bold, hexagonal, upward standing shape on a small foot, and a small fluted shape which has a small four-footed base. This latter shape of foot can be well seen in the site fragment in Plate 2. As the moulded decorations of these vary somewhat in similar examples, it is reasonable to suppose that the early Worcester method of mould-making previously described—pitcher moulds—was also in use at Bristol. Some boats are known which have one side quite different in modelling from the other, suggesting that the worker sticking up the two halves was not too particular which halves of moulds he used.*

The group of ware is only moderately translucent; that is, the pieces do not show a great deal of light through their bodies when held up to an artificial light. But such translucency as they do show varies from a thickish blue-green to a clearish white. Firing cracks are quite common—generally to be seen around the junctions of handles, by the joints of the two halves of the boats, and under the base. The glaze is very close fitting and never crazes, and there are no signs of the glaze having been wiped off to leave a glaze-free margin. Some of the pieces have workmen's marks—incised marks in the body before firing—which comprise nicks and crosses. They are probably tally marks intended for adding up the total of pieces made by the workmen, who were paid on a piece-rate basis. More will be said about these workmen's marks, especially the scratch crosses.

No painters' marks are found on Bristol marked pieces. These marks, put on by the painter in underglaze-blue to identify his work, exist in dazzling profusion on early Worcester blue and white pieces and will be discussed later. The underglaze-blue on Bristol pieces is rather dark and blotchy, with a slight tinge of indigo. It is typified by the work of the painter who placed

---

* The two halves of these boats always have a suitable motif on the outside of the lip which blends the sides together cleverly.

three large dots in the middle of Chinese landscapes, as will be seen in the left-hand piece in Plate 2. The 'three-dot' painter should not be confused with the later Worcester group of 'cannonball' painters, who also placed three large round dots on the pieces.

It is probable that the three-dot painter (we do not know his name), together with most of the other painters on Bristol and Bristol/Worcester, came to Miller & Lund's factory from one of the very flourishing and numerous delft factories in Bristol. I have seen a number of Bristol delft pieces which could be by the same hands as very similar scenes on porcelain, although the considerable differences in technique required make comparisons very difficult. Certainly the freedom of painting, together with the choice of subject based either on direct copies from the Chinese or at second-hand via the Dutch Delft painters, suggests that most of these early painters came from the delft factories. There was no tradition of earthenware painting in Worcester apart from some local slip decoration, which seems to have been superseded by the Staffordshire imported ware by about 1720.

It is tempting to try to see the hand of Michael Edkins, the Bristol delft painter, on some Bristol/Worcester pieces—especially in some Chinoiserie work in enamels; but it is very difficult to compare the work on such different materials.

Also in Plate 2 is a large sauce-boat which corresponds with Dr. Pococke's description of 'beautiful white sauce boats adorned with reliefs of festoons'. It is high-footed, with flaring rim and protruding lip; and it has a complicated high handle with, on the upper part, a modelled dolphin whose tail forms the thumb-rest. Other similar ones have the moulded festoons picked out in colour, and some of these have been found having the Bristol mark painted over with a green leaf—possibly as an attempt to conceal the place of origin. The likely reason is that these were decorated at Worcester from Bristol made pieces, before fresh moulds were made, in the first years of production, no colour pieces being made at Bristol.

Many boats of similar shape are known with plain loop handles, but none of these is marked with the word 'Bristol'. The finds from the site suggest that these shapes went on being made for quite a long time—until about 1758 —although, as previously explained, it is possible to find numerous examples which are slightly different from each other because of the method of mould-making.

Summing up the 'Bristol' (or 'Bristoll') marked pieces, they comprise the figure of the Chinaman, of which only seven examples are known; small cream- or butter-boats—of low-footed shape, or fluted and with four footed-base, or hexagonal—which are found either in blue and white or with onglaze decoration; and the tall-footed, tall-handled sauce-boats either left in the white or with onglaze decoration. Although the Bristol marked pieces almost invariably have a greyish appearance, it is possible that some of the ware made at Bristol has a creamy look, no creamy-looking pieces being found in the lowest levels of the Warmstry House site. This would agree with Dr. Pococke's description of two types of ware being made at Bristol, as noted on page 6.

Bristol/Worcester

Bristol/Worcester pieces—that is, pieces of similar early or primitive type but not marked 'Bristol'—exist in fairly large numbers and cover an astonishing range of shapes. In general, the body has a greyish look and the translucency varies from a clearish light green, especially in the thinner potted pieces, to a thicker darker green. This green translucency is present in the biscuit fired ware and seems little affected by the glaze. Firing cracks are common, especially around the junctions of handles, where the frequent use of simple spiral decoration is probably a subtle way of disguising them. The glaze is always well fitting and never crazes; and there is no glaze-free margin on bases—a feature that does not seem to occur before 1755 at the earliest. Two noticeable features of the glaze of the earlier ware are that it is generally more tinted with cobalt, giving a greyer, starchier appearance, and black spots are more apparent in patches on the surface. The glaze is applied quite thickly and often pools on the bases of the larger pieces. Chemical analysis of a fragment from the lowest level on the site shows that it contains about 40% of soapstone, about the same as fragments from levels of about 1765 and 1785; so the basic body does not change much over the thirty or more years that are covered by this book.

The shapes are very interesting—mainly based on the Chinese, although some seem to show a Chelsea and Bow influence. Small pieces comprise twelve-sided cups and saucers (Plate 8); cream-boats, similar to the 'Bristol' marked ones, with simple square-shaped handles topped by a small curled knob; other cream-boats with very complicated pagoda scenes in moulded landscape rising uphill towards the handle (Plate 5); cups with four flutes down the body, each flute narrowing from the rim to the base (Plate 15); delicate fluted cups, the tops of the flutes being just below the rim in a curious crenellated formation (Plate 7); beautiful thrown small mugs with slightly spreading flat bases (Plate 14); shallow, straight-sided coffee cans with square handles similar to the 'Bristol' cream-boats; globular mugs with cylindrical necks and bases; thickly potted flat dishes with a flanged rim, for potted meats; and curious little baskets with fluted, lobed sides and a handle across the top.

Larger items include very fine bowls with alternate ribbed and indented flutes; hexagonal small vases with tall necks (Plate 16); and jugs and mugs of a class known as the 'scratch cross group' because they are of a type which frequently has a saltire cross or a nick incised in the base or foot-ring—a general characteristic of this group being that they have strong rounded feet, and handles whose lower terminal curls away from the body and ends in a straight-cut edge. Some mugs with spreading bases can have this latter characteristic. Large jugs of rather bulbous shape and strong spout are fairly common. Tea pots vary from silver shapes with round handles (Plate 10) to fluted or thrown ones of nicely rounded form, having knobs ending in a point or a curious form of indented circle.

Impressed or incised marks made by the workmen—such as crosses or nicks and circles in the bases of turned or handled ware—and decorators' marks in the form of signs, symbols and initials in underglaze blue are quite often found, although not as commonly as upon definite early Worcester pieces.

FIRST PERIOD, OR DR. WALL PERIOD

To deal with this period, which I have presumed to give a span ending at Dr. Wall's death—1751 to 1776—one could either treat the three main forms of decoration—that is, underglaze-blue painted, onglaze painted, and printed— as three distinct subjects and follow each through its separate development, or join the three strands and weave them together through the period. I have decided to use the latter method as being the easiest to comprehend, since it is very clear that there was considerable overlapping of the three elements.

Initially, in 1751, underglaze-blue painting was the chief product of the factory, although early coloured ware was being made in the Meissen style and in the Chinese 'famille verte' and 'famille rose' styles. By 1757 onglaze printing, followed by underglaze-blue printing, began to be just as important as painted ware. In the 1760s the fine coloured ware in the Oriental Arita, Kakiemon and other styles flourished, many of them using some underglaze blue in their decoration, to be followed by the early ground colours of pink and yellow and scale blue in the London style, which speedily developed with the advent of the Chelsea painters in 1768 and the ware decorated at Giles' studio in London—the greatest flowering seeming to come about 1769–70. From this time, there appears to have been a quick turning away from splendidly coloured ware and a move to either a much simpler form of onglaze colours or just gilding or simple underglaze-blue painting, with the rapid growth of underglaze-blue printing in a violet tone in about 1780 leading into the Davis/Flight period.

As mentioned, a great deal of overlapping took place. For example, in one outstanding group of decorated biscuit ware found on the site—which can be dated about 1770 and consisted of the wasters from the glazing room—there was cobalt painted ware which could well have come from the 1750s; Oriental-type ware of the 1760s; underglaze printing of such patterns as the 'fence' and various flower scenes; scale blue ware; fine pieces in the white, ready for onglaze grounds or painting at Worcester or in London; and late underglaze-blue painting which would be generally thought of as the late 1770s. The shapes varied from moulded sauce-boats of the 1750s to fine chocolate-cups of the 1770s. Thus, a range of ware which would be generally thought to span a period of twenty years was all obviously contemporary; and the finding of levels like this makes nonsense of any attempt to date a piece closely.

Two major factors contribute to this difficulty of dating ware of the Dr. Wall Period, especially the blue and white pieces: the body seems to have changed hardly at all between 1755 and 1776, so there is no certain way of telling the date of a piece by the material; and certain patterns continued to be popular throughout most of the period, painted by artists who were trained to paint a certain scene and went on doing it for fifteen or twenty years.

After the initial difficulties of manufacture of the first two or three years had been overcome, the general standard of production was kept at such a high level until, at any rate, 1776 that I am convinced it is impossible to date the ware of this period to within a few years.

The most accurate guide to dating must be the sequence of introduction of a certain shape or pattern by its finding on the site in the earliest level in which it appears and relating this to the few dated pieces that are in existence. This is the method which I propose to follow in dealing with the ware.

Early Period, 1751 to 1755

There are not many dated pieces from the first few years of Worcester. The piece with the earliest date is a small mug, $3\frac{5}{8}$ inches tall, with a spreading base and a handle of the type previously referred to as the scratch cross family, with a cross incised in the base (Plate 6). Known as the 'Tracy Mug', it shows a scene on each side of the handle depicting 'Conquest' and 'Gratitude', divided by a centre inscribed column on a pedestal referring to a Parliamentary election in Worcester in 1747, when Robert Tracy was elected to Parliament following an extraordinary reversal of the original result. The pedestal is painted with the inscription 'Erected to commemorate ye gratitude Freemen of Worcester owe Robert Tracy Esq., who restored their Liberty by defeating an arbitary power in the year 1747'. The painting, in onglaze colours, was done by a hand unused to porcelain painting and is very similar to a number of paintings on canvas of classical figures by Dr. John Wall himself which are in the Perrins Museum. John Wall was a friend of Robert Tracy and the mug was painted as a commemorative piece. The question is, when? If done in 1747, this is even before the possible starting date of the Bristol factory; but I feel sure that the piece must have been a belated commemoration, done on a Worcester piece after 1751.

The scratch cross on the base of the mug is similar to a number of such marks on early Worcester pieces and even, as explained, on Bristol marked pieces. It should be made clear that such marks cannot be regarded in any sense as factory marks, and they are found on the ware of other factories besides Worcester. But pieces exactly matching the shape of this mug can safely be regarded as Worcester.

A large white moulded tureen with the date 1751 in underglaze blue is described by R. W. Binns,* but its whereabouts is unknown. If a genuine piece, it certainly shows a remarkably advanced technique for a factory in its initial year of production; although some of the earliest known ware do show a great competence. The British Museum has a cup, inscribed 'T.B. 1753', with a primitive, crudely painted scene. The only other blue and white dated piece from the first ten years of the factory is a miniature sugar bowl, cover and

* *A Century of Potting*, 1877, 2nd edition, p. 23.

stand, inscribed 'C.S. 1758', from a miniature service made for Charlotte Sheriff. This is decorated with the 'prunus-root' pattern.

A number of Bristol shapes continue well into the late 1750s. If decorated in blue and white, the earlier the piece the more likely it is for the blue to be rather blurred in its effect. High-footed sauce-boats, hexagonal cream-boats, and fluted and hexagonal cups are fairly common shapes, often having elaborate moulded rococo scrolls which are not always clearly seen when covered with glaze. The fine modelling may be observed more easily on the unglazed fragments from the site. The boats often have elaborate curved thumb-rests, and some two-handled sauce-boats have the thumb-rests moulded as monkey-heads. Where panels are left surrounded by scrolls, decorations of all sorts can be found, ranging from mainly Oriental types of flowers to scenes. These can be in blue and white or in onglaze colours in a rather restricted palette, sometimes copying famille verte and famille rouge or with very simple prints of a rather smoky grey colour—a long way removed from the splendid black colour of the great 'jet enamel' prints to come later.

These early prints, known as the 'smoky primitives', are delightful little scenes showing such things as squirrels or battleships. Great controversy exists over who actually originally introduced printing to Worcester—Robert Hancock, Richard Holdship, or the mysterious outsider Boitard. Whether this question will ever be decided, as also the question of whether Worcester or Bow was the first factory to start printing on porcelain, may best be left to be thrashed out elsewhere, recording here only proved facts. Certain it is that these primitive prints are a long way removed from the fine King of Prussia prints, which are dated 1757, and the other very fine early prints of King George II and other worthies of the day.

The smoky primitive prints were generally put in the small reserve panels of the early sauce-boats and cream-boats of silver shape; and most of the moulded vessels of these first few years are of silver shape, some of them quite possibly produced in pitcher moulds from an actual silver vessel impression. These vessels range from cups with square handles and elaborate fluted bodies, bleeding-bowls with scrolled shell-shape handles, and single- and double-lipped sauce-boats to huge tureens, some of them having a finial in the form of a dolphin (Plate 18). Decoration can be in blue and white with small landscape scenes—often with small Chinese figures or strange birds—or simple onglaze landscape or floral scenes.

Large jugs, either round-necked or with lips, are usually decorated in onglaze colours, such as the magnificent pair made for the Corporation of Worcester with the City arms painted on them and dated 1757. The mask jugs seem to overlap the round-necked jugs. Both use a motif of moulded cabbage leaves for the body, and the shape is probably one of the most characteristic that Worcester produced, although also copied by other factories. The mask—the modelling on which can be very clearly seen in the biscuit waster shown in Plate 42—exists in two main forms, one having a taller and more elaborate section at the top of the mask. The detail of the mask should be carefully examined, as both Caughley and Lowestoft made variants. The Worcester mask has a benign expression, with eyes sleepily closed and few furrows in the brows.

Early teapots can have a variety of knobs to the covers. One type has a knob of mushroom shape with a depressed round ring in the top* (this was found in the earliest level on the site); another is in the form of a twig.† But the most common knob is like an inverted top, and this version runs through most of the Dr. Wall period, although it was to have a great rival in the beautiful flower knob which was in use by about 1757. Teapots are among the finest objects that Worcester produced. Not only are they always aesthetically pleasing in shape, with spouts and handles perfectly in proportion and balance, but they are also the most practical of shapes, the positioning and angle of the spout producing a perfect vehicle for pouring. The teapots have from four to eight pierced strainer holes at the base of the spout arranged in a haphazard formation, unlike the accurate geometric positioning characteristic of Lowestoft, although a common formation is an oval shape (Plate 28).

Large octagonal dishes of about thirteen inches in length, decorated with flowers and rocks in underglaze blue, are rare—examples being found in the lowest levels only. They were probably not being made after 1755. Other large objects are huge hexagonal flowerpots for bulbs, with a round hole in the centre of the base for drainage (Colour Plate 1), which were meant to rest in a similarly shaped stand, having the same type of cell border and floral painting.

Smaller objects include curious hexagonal vases with bulbous bodies and long necks (Plate 16) which at first are generally decorated in colours with the 'wheatsheaf' pattern and later with prints, and larger hexagonal vases, $10\frac{1}{2}$ inches high, with curious pairs of handles in the form of dragons looking like arms akimbo, which are usually decorated with Chinese-type figures such as the 'Long Eliza'. There are also sweetmeat or pickle dishes in the form of moulded scallop shells; dry-mustard pots with elongated pear-shaped body and conical lid; and sauce-boats of cos lettuce leaf shape with crabstock handle and lip twisting to the left for right-handed pouring. The last mentioned were not found on the site until the further excavations of 1978.

The three types of decoration for this early ware—that is, pieces made up to about 1755 or 1756—were the smoky primitive prints, onglaze enamel painting in the Chinese or Meissen styles and, principally, blue and white underglaze painting of very high quality albeit rather naïve and without the sophistication of the later blue and white.

Dr. Bernard Watney has isolated ten separate blue and white patterns of the early period. Although some of them are now very rare, and not all of them were found on the site, they all occur on definite Worcester shapes and they are briefly described as follows:

1. *The swimming ducks:* two ducks and an arched bridge between islands.
2. *The zig-zag fence:* a zig-zag fence flanked on one side by a peony and on the other by an upright rock out of which grows a flowering prunus.

---

* *English Blue and White*, Watney, Plate 32A.
† *Worcester Porcelain*, Barrett, Plate 9A.

3. *The plantation:* a fence enclosing tall bamboo trees next to a group of upright rock-like posts, and an island formed of humped boulders with a Chinese house. (This grew into an early primitive print.)
4. *The willow-root pattern:* one or two sloping fences, one of which is next to a gnarled willow tree with arched roots; a plant with bent leaves; two mountain peaks with a flag post between them; and, in some versions, a tall Chinese woman and a man fishing from a boat.
5. *The warbler pattern:* a short angled fence abutting on to a rock with circular holes; out of the rock grows a twisted peony plant; a long-tailed 'Ho Ho' type bird stands on a rush with bent leaves; and one or more flying insects.
6. *The prunus-root:* prunus blossom growing from a root—a pattern which was to run for a number of years.
7. *The cormorant:* the cormorant sits on a large rock, watching a man fishing from a boat; a chrysanthemum between two broad leaves. (Not to be confused with the fisherman and cormorant pattern of the Davis/Flight period.)
8. *The tambourine:* a woman playing a side-drum is followed by a male dancer with a tambourine in a steeply sloping landscape with two mountains.
9. *The bridge:* a high rocky island with a house and a willow tree, connected to a smaller island by a bridge; on the bridge is a man with a fishing rod; another man is fishing from a boat.
10. *The crescent moon:* an elaborate scene including an ornamental fence, islands, pagodas, conifers, fishermen in boats, and a crescent moon facing upwards.

As well as the main patterns on pieces, the decorators continued a number of Bristol/Worcester mannerisms: spouts and handles frequently have extra decorations, Chinese precious objects and small leaves on the spouts and small scroll and spiral patterns on the backs of the round handles; small comma-like marks cover up firing cracks, although these are becoming much less common. A frequent addition to scenes is three large dots, but not by the same hand as on the Bristol marked boats. Borders begin to be frequently employed, generally copying Chinese blue and white directly, such as diaper and flowerheads.

This was the great period for the use of painters' marks, found usually under the foot-rings but also under teapot covers, beneath handles, inside sauce- and cream-boats, and even on knobs. The painters' marks were almost certainly intended to be used as tally marks. It has already been mentioned that no painters' marks are found on definite Bristol pieces, and it is also likely that the great majority of blue and white ware with painters' marks emanate from Worcester. Some of the most common marks are variants of a 'TF' monogram, about which there have been a number of suggestions as to their meaning—ranging from Thomas Frye, of the Bow factory, to the initials of the Tonquin Manufactory. Other common marks are one or two arrows through an annulus, three dots in the form of a triangle, and three parallel lines and a 'P'.

The potting of this early ware is always very good and there is remarkably little distortion of shape, except in the largest pieces. Glaze is usually well fitting and never cracks or crazes. A glaze-free margin is occasionally to be seen, although not as frequently as in the ware of the late 1750s and after. Glaze is not found on the underside of the flange of a teapot cover, nor on the base of foot-rings. By artificial light the translucency is generally green of a quiet, gentle colour, varying from a bluish green to a yellowish green.

Middle Period, 1755 to 1768

The early period was, to some extent, exploratory. Shapes and patterns were being developed, the Company was learning to control decorating and firing techniques, and the way was being prepared for a time of rapid expansion in quality and quantity.

The three methods of decoration—blue and white painting, onglaze painting, and printing—took great strides forward. And of the three, the greatest steps were made in printing.

The process of printing on enamels was already a flourishing business by 1753. At one time, it was thought that most of the early work on such objects as snuff boxes and watch-backs was done at Battersea; but recent researches suggest that the main centres were in Bilston and Wednesbury. A number of the smoky primitives had already appeared on enamels, some of them being designed by Boitard and engraved by Robert Hancock in 1754 with the intention of using them for book plates. Possibly Worcester was able to obtain some of these engravings, as they appear on a number of early shapes—but this is purely speculation. It has been suggested, as a possible alternative, that the printing on these pieces was actually done at the enamel works, as Dr. Richard Pococke, writing on August 28th, 1754, records: 'I went to see the china and enamel manufactory at York House, Battersea.'*

Robert Hancock went to Worcester towards the end of 1756, and by the next year were produced the splendid onglaze prints of the King of Prussia, the great hero of the day, some of them actually carrying the year '1757' on the engraving.† The quality of the 'King of Prussia' prints and the other onglaze prints of well known people such as King George II and III, Queen Charlotte, William Pitt, the Marquis of Granby and William Shakespeare, is remarkable and must have taken the public by storm. Known in their time as jet enamels, the wonderful strong black colour of the very best printed pieces, in which the colour sinks in through the glaze, can be quite breathtaking.

Very large quantities of printed pieces must have been made on most of the shapes then current and in a multitude of different scenes, most of the finest bearing the hallmarks of the quality of the 'King of Prussia' print. It is probable that Hancock designed the majority of the best of these, although the claims of Richard Holdship—one of the original Worcester partners—must not be forgotten. It is likely that there are distinctly different hands at work on the design of these prints: the smoky primitives of squirrels, battleships and

* *Travels through England of Dr. Richard Pococke*, 1888, Vol. 2, p. 69.

† Although it is usual to refer to the coppers as having been engraved, it may be as well to point out that most of the coppers for onglaze printing seem to have been etched rather than engraved, although some strengthening by a graver was done after the etching had been sufficiently bitten into by acid. However, underglaze printing was probably done from engraved coppers.

the four seasons; the other primitives of the zig-zag fence, the plantation, swans and other birds; and the remainder which are probably Hancock's work. The middle group of primitive type, some of which were also used as the first of the underglaze prints, could well be by Richard Holdship. It is tempting to see the possible demoting of these from onglaze to underglaze as the cause of Holdship's leaving Worcester and going to Derby in 1764, the appearance of versions of these prints on later Derby pieces supporting this idea.

Leaving speculation aside, the main bulk of the finest prints are certainly by Hancock and cover a multitude of subjects, from the 'heroes' already mentioned to attractive garden scenes such as the 'tea party' and 'l'amour', country scenes like 'draw-well' and 'milkmaids', chinoiseries of 'siesta' and 'les garçons chinois', splendidly stirring hunting scenes on punch bowls, masonic scenes and elaborate creations of classical ruins.

In recent years, it has been felt that there is something inferior about prints on porcelain—that they are a second-rate, cheaper, mass-produced method of decoration. This feeling is a relic from the early years of this century, when the only really collectable ware was the coloured grounds. But this view has changed a lot lately, and printed and blue and white ware are being looked at with more understanding.

Printed ware was not regarded as being a second-rate form of decoration in the eighteenth century, and it was probably no cheaper than the other forms of decoration when they were introduced. In fact, it was regarded as such a great invention and novelty that it could well have cost more initially. It is wrong to try to compare transfer printing with painting. One might as well try to compare an orange with an apple. They are two completely different things. The more elaborate scenes come off splendidly when engraved and printed; but most of them would be impossibly clumsy if painted—for instance the 'draw-well' (Plate 37).

The prints were put on most of the current shapes, including even the large and elaborately handled vases (Plate 46). These vases were to be the ones used by Donaldson and O'Neale (Plate 83) for the finest possible onglaze decorations, and it is a pointer to the high regard in which printing was held that they were thought worthy to go on to the more expensive ornamental pieces. The most effective use of prints was on large curved surfaces—such as bowls, mugs and vases—where the effect of the print shows that great care had been taken in designing the engraving to fit the particular shape. The least effective use of prints was on moulded ware, where the print often had to cross the various sections of the moulded pattern.

Frequently, groups of different prints were put on one vessel—particularly jugs, mugs and vases, which would often have two or three different scenes around them. An example of this is a mug in the Perrins Museum which has three prints on the body. There is a 'bonus' print under the base of the mug, where there are also the imperfectly fired-away remains of numbers (Roman and English) which were probably directives to the workman as to where to place the particular print. These numbers—which are in vegetable dyes and

should have fired away but through some extraordinary mischance have remained to us—would possibly have been put on by the printing foreman, or
even by Hancock himself, and show the great care that was taken in planning
the use of the prints.

One of the great charms in the collecting of printed ware lies in the different
combinations of the scenes on one vessel. Others are the large variety of these
scenes, and the many subtle differences in the way that smaller groups of
subsidiary prints can be arranged: for example, the way in which the 'King of
Prussia' print can have different subsidiary prints of 'Fame', 'Conquest' etc.,
and different battle honours added, reflecting the King's successes in the war.
Large numbers of versions of the more popular prints exist—for example, the
'tea party' can vary by the addition or deletion of a servant in the background
or the dog in the foreground, or in changes in position of the main characters.

A great many onglaze prints were coloured in by washes of enamel colours.
These are not to be confused with 'clobbered' ware, which are blue and white
underglaze painted pieces having enamelled colours—generally reds, greens
and gilding—overlaid on the glaze in an attempt to make the basically simple
decoration look rich and so sell for a greater price. More is said about clobbering in Chapter V.

The genuine coloured-over ware can be very charming when the colours are
applied with sensitivity, as they usually are. As this process is to be seen on
some of the shapes of the mid 1750s and associated with some of the smoky
primitives, we can assume that it was brought in soon after the first use of
printing at Worcester. Colouring-over can appear on most of the onglaze
prints—for instance, on a mug commemorating the death of General Wolfe, on
a 'tea party' cup and saucer, cauliflower tureens, and teapots with armorials.
The most spectacular pieces in this form are cabbage leaf mask jugs printed
with elaborate country scenes of 'May Day' or 'Milkmaids' coloured over,
the spaces between the prints filled with ground colours of yellow and green
(Colour Plate II). Dishes and bowls can be finished in the same way. It is often
suggested that a number of these were done at Giles' decorating studio. While
this may be possible, there is no proof of it.

The other type of coloured onglaze prints—that is, those with a decoration
printed in black outlines and filled in by hand with enamels, almost in the
style of a child's colouring book—would appear to be later than the coloured-
over prints, probably not appearing until the early 1760s. Typical of this ware
are 'the red cow' and 'les garçons chinois' prints. The obvious intention was
to provide basic, easily coloured pieces which could be done by young
apprentices or girls. There is the likelihood that Giles bought some of these,
and this has led a number of authors to ascribe all the coloured-in ware to
Giles' studios. It has always seemed to me unlikely that the Company would
have gone to the labour of producing ware up to the stage of requiring
simple filling in, which would turn a cheaper priced piece into a richer item,
and leave an outsider to receive the quick profit that such colouring would
produce. Worcester undoubtedly would have had a large number of young
and inexperienced painters perfectly able to do such simple work—a type of

painting that most English porcelain and china factories have done internally from the eighteenth century to this day. Failing proof, I feel it is safer to ascribe the majority of this type of coloured work to Worcester.

Very few of the onglaze printed pieces bear a factory mark. It would appear that the main factory mark of the crescent was not engraved on the copper plates intended for onglaze printing. In fact, the crescent and the various forms of 'W' do not appear to have been used until the very late 1750s, by which time the use of transfer printing was well established. Even the printed ware made after factory marks became the practice generally do not have them. This can be explained by the fact that pieces found suitable for onglaze printing following the biscuit firing would be sent direct to the glazing department for glazing and subsequent firing in the glost kiln and then on to the printing department. By then fully glazed, there was obviously no chance of putting on underglaze marks.

Underglaze printed pieces, on the other hand, generally have printed crescent marks on their bases. The process of printing underglaze was first employed much later in period than onglaze. The earliest underglaze pieces appear in levels that would be dated about 1758, and they would presumably date from about that time. The first underglaze printing discovered is of relatively poor quality compared with the contemporary onglaze work, comprising some simple floral patterns, and a Chinese scene, of a 'man in the pavilion watching a boat' pattern. For the first few years up to 1760, these few prints were the only underglaze prints to be done and their quality cannot be compared with that of the fine blue and white underglaze painting of the same period.

The underglaze prints of this period are found on most of the current shapes: straight mugs, bell-shaped tankards, D-ended bough pots, chamber pots and mask jugs. The earliest underglaze printing shows the same troubles as the earliest blue and white painting, with running and blotching of the cobalt. But with this conquered, the floral prints in particular could be very beautiful. The growing quality of underglaze printing led to its use on the most important of pieces—for instance, on the modelled dish (Plate 41) and the ornamental vase (Plate 46), vessels which would normally have been decorated by the finest onglaze painting. By 1770 or so, most of the onglaze printing had been ousted by underglaze, which now was being made in enormous quantities and of great quality.

One great dumping of wasters of about 1770, already referred to, contained a large quantity of the 'Fence' pattern (Plate 134) and it has been possible to show that two coppers were in use for the smallest sized tea bowls, four for the normal sized tea bowls and two or three for most of the other tea and coffee ware such as saucers, coffee cups and cans. Four copper plates can produce a vast amount of pieces in a day, and the finding of such evidence in an obviously contemporary group is proof of the tremendous demand that the production of such ware had to satisfy.

Although a few years remained before the death of Dr. Wall and the introduction of the later 'disguised numeral' prints of the Davis/Flight period, a number of new prints were introduced. Varied floral scenes based on delft blue and white painting are common; the use on underglaze of some of the onglaze prints with scenes of the 'tea party' and King George can be found but rarely.

Underglaze printed ware is generally marked, as distinct from the general lack of marks on onglaze printed ware. The most commonly used mark of this period on underglazed printed pieces was a crescent, which was itself printed and can appear in a number of different forms—from a crescent with lines running horizontally filling the inside, to one with an inner line, either hatched in or not. The hatching appears to have been added to the crescent when the copper went back to the engraver for repair, a crescent with a line probably indicating a print from the original copper. Sometimes, the crescent can have an addition of a letter—for instance, an 'E', 'L' or 'R' to the right of the open part of the crescent. These are rare and it is impossible to be certain of their meaning, although they could refer to foremen of different printing shops. The rarest form of addition is the filling up of the crescent with the face of a man-in-the-moon, a mark found in a pit which probably dates from about 1770. One of the forms of the 'W' mark could also be used on this ware, although by no means as frequently as a crescent; and very occasionally a square mark may be used.

It should be stressed that the hatched crescent mark is almost certainly exclusive to Worcester, although the open crescent was used on Lowestoft.*

ONGLAZE COLOUR PAINTING OF THE DR. WALL PERIOD

Onglaze painting, including ware that has onglaze enamels over a basic underglaze cobalt blue painting—such as the scale blue and 'Queen Charlotte' patterns—fall fairly naturally into three main groups and periods. These are

(1) Early paintings up to about 1760.
(2) Oriental-type copies of Chinese and Japanese painting of about 1760 to about 1768.
(3) European-type painting, with or without grounds, of about 1768 to 1776.

Although these types of onglaze decoration form three distinct groups, the periods outlined above can only be regarded as the ones in which the particular forms of decoration were most common; and it must be made very clear that there is a considerable degree of overlapping. Especially is this true of the Oriental and European periods. Two pits found on the site contained large quantities of ware of both types, especially scale blue pieces which can be found with either one or the other type of decoration.

* See the companion volume *Illustrated Guide to Lowestoft Porcelain,* by Geoffrey Godden, 1969.

Early Colours up to 1760

The earliest Worcester—not Bristol/Worcester—onglaze decoration would seem to be based much more upon a European style than a Chinese style. Looking afresh at all the ware, including blue and white, definitely made at Worcester up to around 1760—especially after the experience of being able to examine the painting in the unglazed state—has led me to the conclusion that the blue and white paintings are based upon English and Dutch delft painting and the coloured ware mainly upon French and German porcelain and, to a small extent, upon delft. It was not until after 1760 that the decorations became direct copies of Oriental ones—for example, the blue and white ware in Plates 100 and 101 and the coloured ware in Plates 53 to 58.

I realise that this goes against the general idea that most early Worcester had a basic Chinese influence. But if one looks carefully at ware of this period, it is clear that the figures, landscapes and flowers are not really direct copying from the Chinese; rather are they a Chinoiserie owing much more to the influence of delft painters, especially those of the Bristol factories. (As previously mentioned, it is more than likely that most of Worcester's early painters came from Bristol delft factories.)

It is interesting to note that when direct Chinese and Japanese copying did become popular, from about 1760, the coloured ware were copied from the Ch'ien Lung period and contemporary Japanese patterns, but the blue and white—which are much rarer—were from Chinese painting of the much earlier Kang Hsi period and could well have been replacements for Chinese services.

The early onglaze paintings are generally flower painting in the Meissen style (the so-called 'Meissner Blumen'), Chinoiserie, or European landscapes and curious birds of a very primitive type. The shapes include a number that have been placed in the Bristol/Worcester period—the small and larger vases with pairs of handles looking like arms akimbo (Plate 13); mugs of three main forms—with swelling base of scratched cross type, straight sided, and bell shaped; small cream- or butter-boats with square-shaped handle topped with a little round knob; and high-footed sauce-boats of silver shape. Large round-necked jugs are usually reserved for the most splendid decorations—great landscape scenes and armorials, such as the pair of jugs made for the Corporation of Worcester and dated 1757—and the mask jugs can be well decorated, both types of jug being made either with moulded cabbage leaves for the body or of plain shape. Round-bellied vases with short round neck and foot are often decorated with strange birds, such as owls and birds with long curving beaks (Plate 29). Birds are very popular subjects, although they are a long way removed from the later fabulous birds and those painted by Giles or other London decorators.

One bell-shaped mug in the British Museum has a painting of a prim bird with a long tail, perched on a rock, with smaller English-type birds watching from a fence and tree. It is signed beneath the foot 'J. Rogers Pinxit 1757'.

Rogers thus becomes the first of the named painters whose work is found on Worcester and he probably painted a large number of the important scenes of the period and certainly also the Corporation of Worcester jugs, the date '1757' on the three pieces clearly being by the same hand. For an account of this painter and his work, the reader is referred to an article by Hugh Tait, 'James Rogers—A leading porcelain painter at Worcester c. 1755–1765', in *The Connoisseur*, Vol. CXLIX, No. 602 of April 1962.

Relatively little tea ware in onglaze colours seems to come from this period. Such ware was more usually decorated in underglaze blue or onglaze prints, the coloured ware up to and about 1760 generally being rather more ornamental than useful—or at any rate, ornamentally useful. One of the most flamboyant shapes is a flower-holder, sometimes referred to as a crocus-pot or bough-pot (Plate 78) in the rococo style, which first appears near the end of this period decorated with painted birds and is later found with underglaze printed flowers and also the scale blue decoration and fabulous birds.

Oriental- and London-Style Ware of About 1760 to 1768

In this period, some of the most colourful English porcelain of the eighteenth century was made. As well as copies of contemporary Chinese and Japanese coloured patterns, and the introduction of pink scale and blue scale decoration and the early ground colours, a quantity of ware was decorated at Giles' studio in London.

The Oriental patterns are generally direct copies of Chinese and Japanese ones, most of the Japanese copies being from Imari, Kakiemon and Arita types. A great many different patterns are known, and they must have been very popular in the eighteenth century. They are found on the site in levels spanning quite a few years, but the largest quantity was found in a pit that might be dated 1760 or shortly afterwards. A number of them involve the use of underglaze cobalt blue, finished off in onglaze colours. This can vary from solid blue grounds reserving fan-, mirror- or vase-shaped reserves painted with prunus looking like jam-tarts to vertical bands dividing the vessel into panels containing painted flowers, with more flowers in small round reserves left white on the blue bands; from beautifully simple patterns such as the 'fan' to the excitement of the swirling colours of the 'Queen Charlotte' or 'Catherine Wheel' pattern.

Other Oriental-type patterns can be decorated entirely onglaze, such as the 'Bishop Sumner' pattern or the scenes of Chinese peoples; can copy Mandarin or Jesuit type patterns; can have decorations placed on or over moulded patterns, such as puce monochrome paintings on the 'Blind Earl' pattern or painted Chinese figures over feather moulded patterns.

A large number of them have titles, some of which can be confusing as they are sometimes differently referred to in books and auction catalogues. The titles are based either upon those given in the London sale catalogue of 1769, such as 'Old Mosaic Japan' and 'fine old Japan fan' pattern, or after the names of famous people who have possessed pieces, such as 'Sir Joshua Reynolds' and 'Bishop Sumner'.

One range is described as 'pencilled', although the decorations are actually painted with very fine lines. The paintings can be of great delicacy and are often very humorous, with scenes of Chinese and Japanese figures which can look very like onglaze black printed scenes, so finely painted are the lines.

Most of these patterns are painted on shapes which can also be used for European type onglaze colours; but some shapes are reserved exclusively for Oriental paintings, such as the very tall octagonal vases with wide necks and bulbous square projection in an archaic bronze beaker shape (height $16\frac{1}{4}$ and $21\frac{1}{2}$ inches). Scenes that would normally be thought of as European, such as a spirited impression of Joseph fleeing from Potiphar's wife, are given an Oriental slant by painting in a Chinese or Japanese style. The marks are usually squares, although some patterns have groups of Chinese marks arranged inside a double circle.

The European-style paintings of this period were generally based upon Meissen and Sèvres, or London versions of them—although the Worcester work was seldom pure copying. An innate and well developed artistic sense enabled Worcester to absorb different styles and produce something that was entirely and uniquely its own. A sure eye for shape and high quality gilding characterise all the ware of this period, which shows the gradual leading up to a climax by 1768 and for a few years afterwards, when Worcester can undoubtedly be said to have produced the finest porcelain made in this country in the eighteenth century.

The 1760s began with indications of the great pieces that were to come. The use of pink scale would appear to date from 1761, as witness a mug in the Perrins Museum inscribed with that date and the name 'Henry Cook', but this is probably a later decorated piece. Underglaze scale blue was undoubtedly being competently done by then, and quantities were found in a pit which would probably date from about 1760. Scale blue pieces can have either Oriental or European type onglaze decoration—the European varying from well painted English flowers to the exotic quality of the 'fabulous birds'. Yellow as a ground colour and yellow scale—a very rare effect—was almost certainly done by 1761, probably by 1760. Although there are no dated pieces, yellow occurs on a number of shapes that are basically earlier than those on which most of the other grounds appear, and it can vary from a lemon to a sulphur colour.

By the time of the two large auction sales of Worcester porcelain held in London in 1769, the whole range of ground colours was fully in production. The advertisement for the May sale announced that the porcelain was decorated 'in the beautiful Colours of Mazarine Blue and Gold, Sky blue, Pea Green, French green, Sea green, Purple, Scarlet and Gold'. No catalogue of this sale exists, but in the catalogue for the December sale are mentioned such lots as 'Three scarlet ground imag'd jars and two beakers'; 'Four enamelled yellow ground sauce boats'; 'Mazarine blue and gold, wheat-sheaf pattern';

'ditto enamelled in birds'; 'ditto and gold, all enamelled in flowers'; 'A set of three elegant jars and covers of the very rich mazarine blue and gold beautifully enamell'd in birds and insects'; and 'Fine old rich dragon pattern, blue Celeste borders'. The catalogue mentions a large number of Oriental patterns, showing that they were still popular in the late 1760s.

It is difficult to know now precisely what some of the colours were, especially the different shades of green referred to. Green is generally called 'apple green' nowadays, but this term was not mentioned in 1769. The so-called apple green should be correctly referred to as the 'pea green' of 1769, although it will be hard to change such a long standing description. This colour, which was peculiar in that it would not take gilding directly on top of it,* can present a rather too heavy appearance, especially in its darker, more blotchy forms (Plate 68). The 'sky blue' is presumably also the one referred to as 'blue Celeste' and is really a turquoise deriving from copies of Sèvres or Chelsea. This beautiful colour is found in an all-over ground colour but more frequently as borders, when it is often enriched with decoration and gilding. 'Purple', or 'plum', is virtually unknown nowadays as a ground colour, although it is occasionally found in borders. 'Scarlet' would be now known as claret and, while not quite the shade of the claret of Meissen and Sèvres which it was probably trying to emulate, it is still a stirring colour. Blues vary from underglaze scale blue to wet or *gros* blue and powder blue—the stippled appearance of the latter obtained by blowing or dusting the colour on to a prepared surface in a dry powder.

The colours mentioned in the sale detail a number of onglaze scale colours such as a rare brick red, the pink already mentioned, purple peacock, and—rarest of all—red and yellow scale. Lilac is very rare as a ground colour, found only on a bell-shaped mug. Orange is found broken up by gilt or diaper and sometimes in bands, with mons breaking up what would otherwise be too strong a colour to be left on its own. Shagreen—or 'fish roe', as it was called by the Chinese—can have a turquoise or green base; but shagreen should strictly be used to refer to the green form, which gives an impression of being similar to its namesake—a piece of green-coloured sharkskin. The turquoise form should correctly be referred to as 'matrix'.

For illustrations in colour of a number of these grounds, the reader is referred to the beautifully-produced book by H. Rissik Marshall, *Coloured Worcester Porcelain of the First Period*, 1954. Although I cannot agree with a number of the descriptions of manufacturing processes or conclusions, the book contains such a fantastic assembly of illustrations of coloured Worcester pieces that it should be at the bedside of everyone interested in the subject.

Here we must discuss the problem of how much of Worcester's ware was, at this period, actually decorated at the enamelling studio of James Giles in London. It was not uncommon, of course, for outside decorators to buy ware in the white, or partly decorated, and provide additional onglaze colours with the intention of making the ware richer and selling it at a profit. This

---

* Yellow and pink grounds, similarly, do not generally have gilding actually on the ground.

was actually done in Worcester itself by Chamberlain in the third quarter of the eighteenth century, and by Sparks and others in the nineteenth century.

Giles' account books for the years 1771–76 show that he had accounts with a number of factories, including William Davis & Co. of Worcester (the Worcester Porcelain Company) and Thomas Turner of Worcester (later of Caughley). From Worcester he bought a large amount of white ware, and also blue and white ware—undoubtedly ware with underglaze scale or solid blue decoration. It should be clearly realised that underglaze decoration and marks would have been done at the factory, the ware glost-fired and then sent to Giles for the addition of onglaze colours in the white reserves. This process can be seen in Plate 73, the waster from the site on the left having gros blue underglaze colour, covered with glaze and refired, thus leaving a central circular panel which, had it not been a waster, would have been decorated onglaze either in the enamelling rooms at Worcester or at Giles' studios.

The difficulty in deciding which is Worcester and which is London enamelling is very great. With the capture of a number of Chelsea painters by 1768 and the arrival in Worcester of the great decorator O'Neale by the same year, the factory must have had several painters perfectly able to produce ware in the London style and of equivalent quality.

Types of decoration usually ascribed to Giles are based upon the suggestions of Honey, Hobson and Drane that paintings by the same hand upon ware of different factories, including imported Chinese ware, could be the work of an outside decorator. These included characteristics which were referred to as dishevelled birds, landscapes with buildings in green and black, and bird paintings by the 'wet brush painter'. The presentation to the Victoria and Albert Museum of four Worcester plates in 1935 by Mrs. Dora Edgell Grubbe, a descendant of Giles, helped to clarify the position. It was a family legend that the plates were painted by Giles on the occasion of his daughter's marriage. If they are authentic—and there is some element of doubt—they provide a useful corpus of the sort of decoration to be expected from Giles' studio.*

The subjects of the Grubbe plates are:

1. A blue, carmine and gold scale cornucopia-shaped border with central fruit and flower painting, the fruit including a sliced lemon. There are also two mushrooms.
2. Landscape with figures painted in carmine, with flowers on the rim.
3. Landscape with figures painted in green and black, with delicate gilt border.
4. A blue and gilt border with green and blue festoons enclosing a group of dead game, and three smaller groups of animals on the rim.

The first three plates are possibly by the same hand—a painter who has

* These may be seen in H. Rissik Marshall's *Coloured Worcester Porcelain of the First Period*, Ceramic Book Company.

become known as the 'sliced fruit painter', to whom has also been attributed most of the other forms of suggested Giles' decoration, such as:

Landscapes in carmine or green monochrome.
Tenniers-type figure (Plate 63).
Sliced-fruit scenes (Plate 71).
Tulip with 'divergent' petals.
Armorials.
Figure Subjects (Plate 79).
Coloured transfers (Colour Plate II).

If one man had decorated the very considerable quantity of ware of the foregoing type that is still in existence, he would undoubtedly rank as the most prolific porcelain decorator of all time. It is likely that we have a situation similar to that with the underglaze blue and white scene involving three large round dots, painted by the 'cannon ball painter'. It is now certain that there was not just one cannon ball painter but a large number of them, the different hands being very obvious at the unglazed stage. Certain it is that the quality of painting on the probable London decorated pieces described above varies enormously, few of the pieces matching the incredible standard of the Duke of Gloucester service (Colour Plate IV), now thought to be decorated at Worcester.

Other types of decoration usually ascribed to Giles are the wavy gilt pattern, known as the 'Queen's pattern', and gilding involving very broad leaves—such as on the Lady Mary Wortley Montague service (Plate 80).

It is very likely that a lot of this generally accepted London decorated work was actually done at Worcester; but as the discoveries on the site have not helped on this point, I can only leave the matter open.

In this period the influence of London becomes obvious, not only in the style of decoration but also in the shapes and objects that were being produced. A number of ornamental objects began to make their appearance—or at any rate, ornamentally useful ware: such things as a tureen in the shape of a partridge sitting on its nest (Plate 114), a shape also made at other factories; a tureen in the shape of a cauliflower (Plate 35), and another in the form of a pair of billing doves; a recumbent cow used as the knob for a covered dish (Plate 49); large two-handled vases, the scrolls on the handles in a rococo style not commonly seen on Worcester (Plate 46); D-shaped flower holders or bough pots (Plate 78); garnitures of vases in the Chelsea style; twisted handles on teapots and coffee pots (Plate 115); ogee-shaped chocolate or caudle cups with pierced handles (Plate 74); embossed patterns such as the 'Blind Earl' (Plate 30)—named after the Earl of Coventry, who lost his sight in a hunting accident . . . but a number of years after Worcester had started making the shape; vases with applied modelled flowers, shells and masks; and the introduction of figures (Colour Plate VI).

The flowered vases and the figures are generally associated with the supposed arrival at Worcester, in about 1768, of the strange 'repairer' (as the builders-up of applied flowers and figures were called) who is usually said to be a Mr. Tebo, from the mark of 'To', 'T' and 'IT' on a number of pieces of these types, including open-work baskets. In fact, no proof exists to link Mr. Tebo, a modeller who worked for Josiah Wedgwood, with the man at Worcester who marked his work as noted above. Research being conducted at the time of writing may suggest another ceramic modeller as the one who designed and assembled the Worcester figures, baskets etc., bearing these marks.

For a long time it was thought that Worcester made no figures during this period, but a number have now been generally accepted and a full description of them will be found in the next chapter. I must point out that I found no fragments of any of the accepted figures on the site, which was a bit disheartening. But it should be kept in mind that the excavation covered only a small section of the site and was probably not near the shop where the repairing would have been done, which would most likely have been in the main Warmstry House.

The accepted figures all show a typical Worcester soapstone body on analysis,* and the finding on the site of the base of a most elaborate figure group (Plate 129) shows that Worcester figures are not only possibilities but fact. Also fact is that there must be a number of other unthought of Worcester ornamental pieces—as, for example, a large tureen in the probable form of a swan, after the style of Meissen, a large fragment of which was also found on the site (Plate 130).

A large number of the London-type ware have no factory mark. The pieces that are marked have either square marks—especially those having a basic underglaze blue pattern—or copies of other factory marks, such as the crossed swords of Meissen, usually with a number '9' or '91' at the base of the swords, or the marks of Sèvres, Chantilly or Chelsea. On the 'Duke of Gloucester' service, an onglaze gold crescent is used. Of the figures, only some have a 'To'-type mark.

The production of this splendid ware must not blind us to the fact that ordinary coloured ware continued to be manufactured throughout the period —ordinary tea and dinner ware, but always beautifully made and decorated. The way was prepared, as 1768 dawned, for the final flowering of great coloured pieces.

Coloured Ware, 1768 to 1776

By 1768 the Chelsea painters had arrived, the London influence was absorbed and, for a few years, many great pieces flowed from the factory. Among the great influences were the painters O'Neale, Donaldson and Duvivier, and it is worth briefly considering each of them and his style of painting.

Jeffryes Hamett O'Neale, an Irishman, had painted for Chelsea a large number of fable and mythology scenes—his favourite subjects. By 1763, he

* *Analysed Specimens of English Porcelain*, Eccles & Rackham.

was exhibiting miniatures at an exhibition of the Society of Artists. He continued exhibiting until 1766. Some time prior to April 1768 he moved to Worcester, where he lived at the house of Mr. Parson, a watchmaker in the High Street, not returning to London until March 1770. He probably returned to work for Nicholas Sprimont and, later, William Duesbury, also doing some work for Josiah Wedgwood. But it is his period at Worcester with which we are concerned.

It is possible that his paintings on Worcester were done as a freelance, and it has been suggested that the fact that so many of his Worcester paintings are signed may indicate that he was not an actual employee of the Company. Be that as it may, his work is of exceptional interest and anyone wishing to delve deeply into it is advised to study the large number of fable and other paintings illustrated in H. Rissik Marshall's *Coloured Worcester Porcelain*.

Major Tapp has summarised the characteristics of O'Neale's painting so well that I cannot do better than quote them as follows:

1. Large banks of blue or mauve cumulus clouds, especially on specimens with panels of considerable size.

2. Landscapes with blue rivers—*divided* cascades, brown or vandyke rocks in the foreground, sometimes with 'crossed' marks on them; row-boats like punts; hills in the distance puce or blue—never mauve; flocks of small birds high in the skies; occasional full-rigged ships; trees horizontally shaded, often gnarled and split or broken off, and an occasional slender birch with each leaf separate in green or red; foliage showing violent contrasts—red or green, but *never yellow* except on hard paste—enamelled over with long curved sweeps of the brush, particularly near the terminals. Nearly all the larger trees have the appearance of having the upper branches bent *downwards* by the wind. The poplars are rather stumpy, never excessively spiky; lichens growing downwards from cliffs or ruins are never dot-stippled.

3. Figures are invariably correct, high lights obtained by *wash*; contrasts in brilliant blue, steel blue, carmine, and pink clothing.

4. Animals with a tendency to *swollen joints* and in fable compositions generally with red protruding tongues.

5. Classical subjects with ruins; obelisks never pointed; urns purposely out of proportion; long-bodied figures, sometimes of peasants, not appropriate to the composition, often humorous, never with 'tricorn' hats, generally in *camaieu rose*.

6. A great sense of humour.

One should not, of course, expect to find more than a few of these characteristics in each painting; and in some of his signed paintings in the Perrins Museum certain of the most characteristic features, such as Vandyke rocks in the foreground, are not present. Colour Plate V shows a number of the above characteristics, and it was thought helpful to illustrate an O'Neale next to a Donaldson so that their very different techniques could be compared on pieces which are so typical of each painter.

John Donaldson was born in 1737 in Edinburgh, became a well known miniaturist, moving to London in 1760 and exhibiting at a number of places, including the Royal Academy. His work appears on a quantity of Chelsea ware, identifiable by his typical monogram signature. There has always been an element of doubt as to whether he actually went to Worcester, but three important points have convinced me that he did.

1. The Perrins Museum possesses a large vase painted by Donaldson which had 'fled' during its first decorating firing—Donaldson, in common with most decorators, using two firings—and the vase was not proceeded with. It is believed to have remained in the factory collection until it was eventually bought by Mr. Dyson Perrins, and it is difficult to believe that the vase would have been returned to the factory from London just to be stored away.
2. The gilding on Donaldson's vases is of the beautifully delicate type so typical of Worcester factory productions but not of London, and it is hardly credible that the vases would have been sent backwards and forwards between the two cities for this to be done.
3. A number of his pieces make use of the typical Worcester factory colour of dry blue enamel, and this again is more likely to have been done at Worcester.

Donaldson's known paintings on Worcester are fewer than O'Neale's, Marshall noting eighteen pieces only. Colour Plate V shows most of his characteristics, which can be summed up as follows:

1. A much more vigorous use of colour than O'Neale.
2. Quite extensive use of a rich puce colour.
3. The cheeks of figures are often stippled and the facial features are very carefully detailed.
4. The lush appearance of foliage.

The example in Colour Plate V is signed with Donaldson's typical J. D. monogram and forms part of a garniture of three shown in Plate 83. All three are signed with Donaldson's monogram, although most books state that only 'Leda and the Swan' is so signed.

Fidelle Duvivier is a painter whose work on Worcester has never been clearly sorted out. He was a typical wanderer around a number of factories, and the only certain paintings on Worcester are two pieces of a tea service—a teapot in the Marshall Collection at Oxford depicting young lovers in a garden beside an urn inscribed with signature and date '1772', and an unsigned cream-jug from the same service in private hands. These may well have been outside decoration as in 1772 Duvivier should have been in a period of employment with Duesbury at Derby, according to an agreement between them which has been preserved.

The splendid type of ware previously described continued to be made during at least the first few years of this the final part of the Dr. Wall period, although the trend seems to have been towards more simple decoration. Instead of ground colours all over the vessel but for the reserved panels, blue borders with painted centres became popular.

Simple floral sprays, occasionally still using dry blue enamels, are common. A delightful form of decoration using a monochrome puce (Colour Plate VIII) is generally most beautifully painted and gilded. A black husk pattern (Plate 131) and the same pattern in gold are typical of this move to simplicity —which was to become even more noticeable in the following Davis/Flight period—the shapes seen in the illustration, with straight flutes and ear-like handles, becoming usual.

It should be stressed again that considerable overlapping takes place and it is possible to find continuing use of scale blue and Oriental colours in this and the next period, perhaps for replacements or for pieces still requiring more splendid decoration.

There is not much dated coloured ware of this time. One mug in the Perrins Museum, although not dated, relates to the Worcester parliamentary election of 1774 when, 'in spite of the Nabob's gold', as the inscription reads, the right candidate won in the end, defeating the bribery of the other party. The decoration of two clasped hands is in dry blue.

A basketwork-like border around plates with twelve indentations is very common (Plate 119), and a favourite form of decoration is the use of classical vases and urns in the Adams style. Straight-sided mugs with blue borders at top and bottom can be decorated with wreaths of flowers or husks enclosing urns and the owner's initials, or crests and coats of arms. Some of the loveliest decoration depicts various kinds of trellises with flowers or hops climbing up them.

Various shapes continued from the previous period. A number of different versions of junket dishes were found on the site and a selection is shown in Plate 95. Wine-coolers became less tub-shaped and more like squat vases, with shell handles at the shoulders. Teapots tended to move away from the round-bodied shape with a foot and a slightly domed cover to a barrel or bullet shape with no visible foot when the pot is standing and a flat cover, still generally with a flower knob.

BLUE AND WHITE PAINTED WARE OF THE DR. WALL PERIOD TO 1776

With underglaze cobalt painted ware, we are now on very much firmer ground than before the excavation since such a great quantity of hardened-on wasters was found on the site. And it is undoubtedly owing to Worcester's extreme care in producing the very finest blue and white possible—thus making extra firing an absolute necessity—that there are so many wasters for us to study.

So huge were the quantities of wasters that a vast amount of information can be obtained about such things as the development of patterns, the number of painters working on the same pattern, and the relative quantities of different patterns being produced at any one time. In company with Peter Ewence and Neal French, two of the Company's designers, I propose to begin a course of study with the eventual aim of producing a treatise on shapes and patterns found on the site and the factory processes. It will be possible, for example, to draw up a complete illustrated catalogue of blue and white patterns, numbered for easy reference.

As a pointer to the useful information obtainable, there follows overleaf a list of standard common borders painted in underglaze-blue (Fig. 4), all found on the site in the biscuit, drawn by Neal French. These borders may be taken as positively proved Worcester ones, although it should be explained that close versions of some of them, especially the diaper borders, occur on other factories' pieces. Here one must take them in conjunction with the main pattern, as it is surprising how consistent is the combination of border and pattern. The borders have been numbered so that they can be referred to in the following description of the patterns.

The last ten borders—numbered 27 to 36—are all found rarely and only one or two examples of biscuit wasters of each were found on the site. Number 27 was found on an osier basket-work bowl, number 28 on a plain shape 3″ bowl associated with a 'prunus root' pattern, number 29 on the inside of a large (8″) 'feather' moulded bowl, number 30 on a printed 'fence' pattern saucer of the 1770s and number 31 on two un-hardened on fragments of 5″ bowls. Number 32 was on a 5″ plate, and number 33 on a 13″ large octagonal dish as illustrated in Watney Plate 28B. Number 34 appears as the border on the 'two quails' pattern and without the dots is used on some Meissen spray patterns, number 35 on late type small oval cream jugs or sauce-boats associated with the Chinese scene with the 'two porters'—men carrying packages—and came from Pits 3 and 4, and number 36 was on straight-sided cups with foliate moulded reserve panels which had landscapes in them.

Blue and white patterns that came after the early years of Worcester are typified by the 'Cannon-ball' scene (Plate 91), so called because of three large round blobs which resemble cannon-balls, but are actually meant to be islands. The scene is really basically a chinoiserie adapted from delft painting, as was probably the Lund's Bristol three-dot painter's scene, but there was not just one cannon-ball painter. There exists a vast quantity of this pattern, and on the site it was shown to have been one of the most popular of the painted scenes. In consequence of its popularity, a great many painters were put to paint it. A number of different hands were discernible on the biscuit wasters in one pit group. It would be illuminating for possessors of a number of pieces of this pattern to examine them minutely to see whether there are differences of technique visible under the blurring effect of the glaze.

The early paintings of the pattern—which occurs on tea and coffee ware—

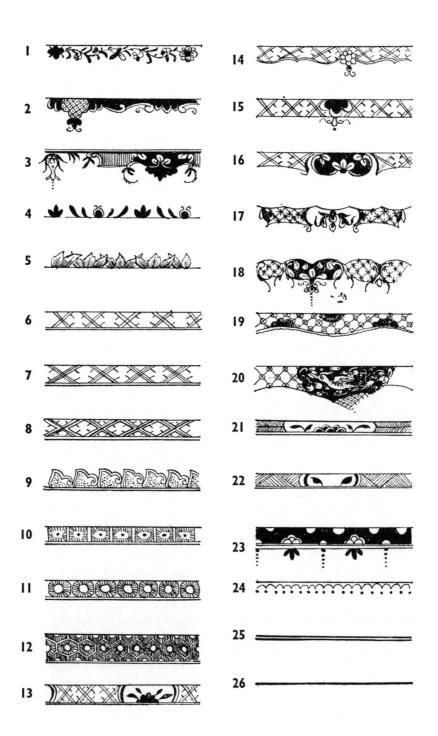

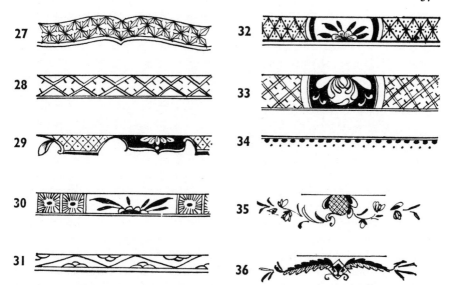

Fig. 4. Painted borders and bands in underglaze-blue found on biscuit ware during dig on Warmstry factory site in 1968.

frequently have painters' marks, and its first introduction could be before 1757. In Pit 4, dating from about 1760, huge quantities of cannon-ball pieces were found, and in Pits 3 and 2 a gradually reducing quantity—as the pattern slowly went out of favour—until by Pit 1, of about 1770, the amount still being made was clearly very small. This shows the long period over which a pattern could be made. The scene always has the same border (number 6), which is also on the 'bird in a ring' pattern (Plate 86).

Another most popular tea and coffee service pattern has beautifully embossed chrysanthemum flowers and sprays (Plate 88). This has two distinct borders: number 3 at the top and 5 at the bottom, or number 8 at the top and 9 at the bottom—the bottom patterns being versions of a chrysanthemum leaf. Versions exist either with or without a great central painted chrysanthemum. The basic quality of the moulded work can vary enormously on different moulds and the bowl shown in Plate 87, although a brilliant piece of modelling, is second-rate compared to some found. The moulded chrysanthemum should be held up to the light to appreciate the full effect of the light showing through the modelling.

The 'chrysanthemum' really shows what a great survival value some patterns could have. First coming in before 1760, it runs right through the Dr. Wall period and turns up again in the Davis/Flight period with one of the late willow pattern prints appearing in the centres, possibly put on a large quantity of old biscuit ware that remained (Plate 137).

A number of patterns continue from the early pre-1755 period, the most popular being the 'prunus-root' pattern (Plate 85). This was found in most of the levels up to Pit 1 in quite considerable quantities. The 'bridge joining two islands', although not very common, runs up to 1770 in a virtually unchanged form. Some patterns go through various changes, with motifs from one joined to motifs from another—examples being the 'plantation' and 'landslip'. A pattern which is now very rare, 'bird in a ring' (Plate 86), was found in a number of levels ranging from about 1760 to 1770. This has border number 6. 'Long Eliza'-type figure paintings continue until shortly after 1760 (Plate 25); but large figure painting seems to fall out of favour until almost 1770, when two fine figure scenes emerge in a much more sophisticated style—a seated lady on a pile of four uncomfortable-looking rocks (Plate 96), and a 'gardener' and another Chinese apparently engaged in an argument about the planting or pulling up of a flower (Plate 103).

A number of smaller figure scenes are found earlier than these, such as those undoubtedly based upon Kang Hsi scenes of a man standing within a double circle surrounded by flowers—a curious version of which, shown in Plate 86, was intended for final onglaze colouring. An exciting hunting scene known as the 'eloping bride', because of the effect of a girl being carried away on the back of her lover's horse with an irate father chasing them on his horse, has a border similar to number 22 but without the bracket panel. Very elaborate Chinese patterns (Plates 100 and 101) and versions of a four-toed dragon with scaled and spiny body are from the few years up to 1770. A strange one-eyed dragon painting was also found.

A large number of painted floral patterns are common, including 'Mansfield'* (Plate 107), which has border number 2. Most of the smaller objects, such as egg-cups and eye-baths, have floral sprays mostly associated with square cell border number 10, as have asparagus servers, pickle trays associated with border number 15, leaf dishes and sauce-boats. Hors d'œuvres sets (Plate 93) are generally painted with florals or a bird on a flowering rock. The so-called Meissen 'onion' or 'immortelle' pattern (Plate 106) is found on ribbed and fluted tea ware, the cobalt on most of these pieces tending to run considerably in the flutes.

A charming scene of two quails (Plate 94), which always has a dotted border, has a long survival value, being found on the site in a level dating after 1780. 'Feather' moulded tea ware having an attractive wavy pattern (Plate 54) usually has floral sprays and border number 1; and straight reed fluted ware has border number 3 at the top and number 4 at the bottom. Powder blue ware with landscape painted reserves (Plate 98) and cracked-ice patterns possibly copy Bow. The 'Chantilly sprig', or gilly flower, is probably a late pattern dating from after 1770 (Plate 125). The 'candle fence and spreading willow' scene (Plate 102) has border number 21 and exists in a different version with a landslip (Plate 86) but without the candle fence. Teacups and saucers with twenty-four flutes ending in points have their own floral pattern (Plate 104) and border number 17. These date from about 1765.

Blue and white dated ware is rare—dates mainly being found on commemoration mugs made for weddings etc.—and seldom has a standard pattern. Most pieces have initials or names and a simple dotted border

---

* This is the title of the modern version of this pattern, previously untitled, made by the Company to this day.

similar to number 24. Such pieces are five mugs in the Perrins Museum, of which three are variously inscribed 'Peter Taylor 1769', 'Frances James 1770' and 'S + B 1776', one—with a scene of St. George and the Dragon—is dated '1776', and the only one having a version of a standard pattern, that of the Cannon-ball but considerably changed and with no border, is marked 'T.A. 1773' under the base.

The finds on the site seem to indicate that after 1770 painted blue and white ware was gradually being dropped in favour of underglaze printed ware. This bears out Binns opinion* that in 1770 there was a serious strike amongst the painters because of the increasing use of transfer prints and that a number of them left the factory. It is possible that the Plymouth factory took the opportunity this presented of advertising in the local paper—the *Berrow's Worcester Journal*, February 22nd, 1770—for a 'number of sober ingenious artists capable of painting in enamel or blue'.

Although a large quantity of blue and white painting was still being done right up to 1776, there is no doubt that the quality of painting was tending to decline—except, possibly, that of a few old painters. But the standard of underglaze printing was rising.

Ware of these last few years of the Dr. Wall period shows a number of features not so commonly seen earlier. There are occasional examples of ground-down bases (Mrs. Powys, on her visit to the factory in 1771, noted that there were workers grinding bases of vessels to make them smooth). The translucency of most pieces is a yellowish green as opposed to the much stronger green of the previous years. A yellowish stain is often to be seen just inside the foot-ring, either in the glaze-free margin or on the glaze. The cobalt blue generally gives a much stronger effect—almost a blued violet colour as opposed to the softer pale blue of earlier periods of which Colour Plate I is a typical example. This deeper blue was to be such an important feature of the Davis/Flight period.

THE DAVIS/FLIGHT PERIOD, 1776 to 1793

This newly defined and named second or middle period of production at Warmstry House—for the definition and naming of which I take full responsibility—is the one which must obviously cause the most controversy. I realise that those who have been involved in buying or selling eighteenth century porcelain for a number of years will find it very hard to believe that Worcester made all the printed ware marked with the curious 'disguised Chinese numeral' marks, the strange un-Worcester-like violet-blue prints of 'willow pattern' type, prints with hand-washed-in effects, and a body which can have a greyish brown look and a straw or orange translucency—especially in the ware made somewhat after 1780.

I can fully sympathise with anyone who can scarcely credit that this ware is in fact Worcester and not Caughley, in defiance of beliefs held for a

* *First Century of English Porcelain*, 1906.

hundred years. Little did I think when I started the excavation that a few short months later I was going to have to change so much of what I had been brought up to believe as fact.

Here I must give full credit to the pioneer work of Geoffrey Godden, who, before I had even started the excavation, had been working on the theory that the disguised Chinese numeral marks were Worcester. For a full explanation of the way he arrived at this decision, I would direct you to his volume *Caughley and Worcester Porcelain, 1775–1800*, 1969.

Briefly, his theorising was based on three main points:

(a) Chamberlain's record books, preserved by the Worcester Royal Porcelain Company Ltd., make frequent reference to the purchase of this type of ware from Thomas Flight of Worcester—for example, as in a letter from Chamberlain at Worcester to Turner at Caughley '. . . (send) no more teas P. Boat unless they can be sent at the Worcester price 5/6 . . .'. ['P. Boat', which is the standard abbreviation for Pleasure Boat, was the eighteenth century name for the pattern we now call 'Fisherman' or 'Fisherman and Cormorant' (Plate 136).]

(b) Printed ware marked with an 'S', for Salopian, or a definite capital 'C', for Caughley—which marks were found on the Caughley factory site in the biscuit—differ in a number of important ways from ware marked with a printed hatched crescent or a disguised Chinese numeral (which were found in great numbers on the Worcester site).

(c) No disguised Chinese numeral marks or cross-hatched crescents were found on the Caughley site, nor were there any wasters of a large number of patterns always previously associated with Caughley ware which generally carry numeral or hatched crescent marks.

When I started on the Warmstry House excavation, Geoffrey Godden asked me to keep a particular watch for 'fisherman and cormorant' pattern, disguised numeral marks and ware with an orange translucency; and I must truthfully admit that my reaction was the same as most people's would have been: 'These could *never* be found at Worcester, because they are firm characteristics of Caughley.' However, as all these things began to turn up— first one or two fragments and then in ever increasing numbers—I had perforce to accept the new ascriptions.

It is now beyond dispute—in view of the negative evidence from the Caughley site and the positive evidence from Warmstry House and the Chamberlain record books—that Worcester alone used the disguised Chinese numeral marks and made the types of ware associated with them, and that these lie within the Davis/Flight period. It must be kept clearly in mind that both Caughley and Lowestoft made their versions of some of the Worcester shapes and patterns of this period.*

---

* For comparisons of the ware of Caughley and Lowestoft, see the two books by Geoffrey Godden: *Caughley and Worcester Porcelain*, 1775–1800, 1969, and *The Illustrated Guide to Lowestoft Porcelain*, 1969.

In talking to a number of people experienced in porcelain who were as flabbergasted as I at the discoveries, they were the more prepared to accept all the implications if some explanation as to why Worcester should have made such un-Worcester-like ware could be given. While any reason given could only be conjectural, the likeliest one I can think of is that of competition. There is no doubt that Caughley under Thomas Turner became very successful and either built up or developed a public demand for cheaper printed ware.

Both William Davis and Thomas Flight were very astute businessmen and were not the sort to lie down in the face of competition. Dr. Wall and Robert Hancock, who had played such a great part in building up the high artistic standards that had reached their climax around the years 1768 to 1770, had departed; and it is easy to imagine the remaining partners coming to the realisation that making beautiful vases with splendid ground colours was wonderful for the few wealthy artistic patrons but did not bring in the pennies. As well as the competition from Caughley, the very cheap blue and white Nankin imported ware was drastically undercutting Worcester; and it is a fact that very little dinner ware appears to have been made at Warmstry House in the Davis/Flight period, which suggests that they could not compete in price with the Chinese.

I emphasise that this is only a possible reason for the move into the cheaper market; and while it did not happen overnight, it is clear from Chamberlain's letter quoted above that Worcester was eventually able to get below Caughley's price.

The reason why Worcester used the strange disguised Chinese numeral marks on so many of these pieces is not clear to me. Was the Company hoping to pass them off as Chinese ware? Or was it anxious that the ware should not be recognised as Worcester by the remaining wealthy patrons and therefore used a completely new series of marks far removed from the accepted crescent and square? An interesting line of investigation for somebody.

A large quantity of painted ware, both blue and white and coloured, was still made, of course; and high quality ware was still produced for a declining public demand or as replacements for damaged pieces. Particularly is this true of scale blue, quantities of which were found in the levels containing disguised Chinese numeral pieces.

Coloured ware that carried over from the end of the Dr. Wall into the Davis/Flight period included the puce camaieu flowers and gold (Colour Plate 8), simple gold on white patterns that were to pave the way for the simple patterns of gold and purple flowers on spirally fluted tea ware, usually called Flight but which we found in levels on the site that would be before Flight bought the business in 1783. The old factory mark of a crescent continued throughout the whole of the Davis/Flight period, although the tendency was for the crescent to be smaller on painted ware. Square marks continued to be used on the blue scale pieces and on the 'Queen Charlotte'—one of the Oriental patterns to run on into this period.

Blue and white painted ware to continue from the earlier period included the 'gillyflower' and the 'two quails'. A number of new patterns were brought in, the most notable being 'blue lily' (Plate 142) and 'music', the former being accompanied by fine gilding and the latter resembling music notation on five-line staves. Both of these continued into the Flight & Barr period after 1793, and it was 'blue lily' that King George III ordered when he visited the factory in 1788, its title subsequently changing to 'royal lily'. It has long been terribly difficult to know whether a piece of 'blue lily' should be attributed to the old first period or to Flight after 1783. The finding of the pattern in levels containing at the same time blue scale decoration, blue printed pieces, and traditionally-held Flight spirally fluted pieces explains the difficulties that previously bedevilled a decision. They are, of course, the products of the Davis/Flight period: and so, too, is 'blue lily'!

Some onglaze printing was still done. A number of onglaze prints of ruins are to be found on the typical spiral fluted shapes of this period. Another characteristic shape is a straight fluted tea canister, the sides widening towards the top, with a flattish cover and button knob (Plate 126).

It is the underglaze printed ware that is the most important of this period, however. The one print from 1770 to remain and even gain in popularity is the 'fence'. This pattern was produced in huge quantities, as is evidenced by the number of different coppers in use for the material found in Pit 1. So many repairs were done to these hard worked coppers and so many re-engravings were made that the number of differences between prints must run into hundreds—some of them, however, being very minute. Caughley also did a version of the 'fence' which is very similar to the basic Worcester one; and of the scenes that were done at both factories, this is the hardest to ascribe where there is no factory mark or where, if the blue has blurred, it is difficult to see whether or not the crescent mark is hatched. This pattern has a two-lined painted border, number 25. Geoffrey Godden gives the principal differences in his Caughley book.

Other prints to continue from before 1776 include scenes of sportsmen with guns; a mother with child (or the 'image' pattern, later to be made in a Caughley version); a pattern of strawberries or pine cones and flowers which goes under various titles but which it may be as well to call 'blue sprays'—the name given to the Company's modern version; the 'three flowers' pattern; and 'birds in branches'.

It is not certain when the new bulk of patterns were first produced but it was probably not much before 1776, as they do not appear in any early levels. A brief description of the patterns follows:

(1) 'Bat' or 'Vase' pattern, which comprises a large vase of flowers with a bat-like creature flying above and another to the left. A table with a basket of fruit stands to the right of centre, with an open-work fence running across the design, the whole enclosed by a wide Chinese-style border.

(2) 'Temple' pattern, of willow-pattern type (without a bridge) showing two tall temple-like Chinese-style buildings on an island, with two pairs of figures standing in the foreground, the whole enclosed by a wide Chinese-style ornate border.

(3) 'Bandstand' pattern, of willow-pattern style with a tall Chinese temple on the right, to the left of which is a bandstand-like structure in which stands a man at the top of a flight of steps. A secondary design comprises two islands joined by a bridge, with one figure crossing it.

(4) 'Argument' pattern, of willow-pattern style with a centre apple (?) tree and an open-ended Chinese building on its left; on its right, in an open low-fronted building, there are two figures raising their fists at each other. A secondary design shows a bridge joining two islands, with a figure crossing from right to left. Various ornate, wide, Chinese-style borders enclose this design, and it can often be seen in the centre of chrysanthemum moulded ware. A similar blue printed design is found on Lowestoft porcelain but not on Caughley.

The above four designs are fairly common, but the following four are much more rare.

(5) European ruin and landscape designs, several different versions of which show European figures posed in front of elaborate ruins of classical style with statues. Some of them derive from onglaze prints—for example, the one shown in Plate 137. Attractive and elaborate borders accompany these prints. A related series of prints show landscape subjects, often with a horseman in the foreground, and these are sometimes found on moulded tea ware.

(6) 'Milkmaid' pattern, showing two milkmaids, each with a wooden pail of milk on her head, and a central figure arranged in landscape with cows and farm buildings. A secondary print shows three cows. Similar onglaze prints are found on Worcester porcelains. Some examples bear the initials R. H. (presumably for Robert Hancock), with the place name 'Worcester' or the abbreviation 'Worc'. A cup and saucer in the Schreiber Collection at the Victoria and Albert Museum is signed in full 'Hancock fecit'.

(7) A fruit pattern depicting a central peach, a gooseberry, two cherries, a bunch of round berries or grapes, and three berries on long stalks, surrounded by a border of six-sided Chinese-style diapers.

The patterns listed above do not occur on Caughley porcelains. The following designs are, however, found on the ware of both Worcester and Caughley but are printed from different copper-plates and display variations in subject and technique which are consistent. It is usually an easy matter to decide from which factory a piece comes.

(8) 'Fisherman' or 'Fisherman and Cormorant' pattern, called in contemporary accounts 'Pleasure Boat', showing a Chinese man standing on the stern of a large sailing boat holding a fish in his hand, which presumably has been caught for him by the cormorant who perches with wings outspread on a large rock to the left. A secondary print shows a seated man, with a feather in his cap, fishing with rod and line from a rock. This has a standard border of square cells and inside this another border, usually referred to as 'dagger' or 'fleur de lys' but actually made up of three large round dots arranged like an upside-down triangle. The Worcester version may be easily differentiated by a number of points, the chief ones being that the fishing line of the little seated fisherman wiggles as if in the wind and goes deep down into the water, whereas the Caughley version has a perfectly straight line which stops at the water line; the three dots of the Worcester version are hatched across with closely engraved parallel lines, whereas the Caughley dots are solid; the main fisherman on the Worcester is of good proportions and the fish is long and

F

slender, whereas the Caughley fisherman is disproportionately tall and stringy and holds a poorly engraved plump fish. A number of other minor differences may be observed in the comparative photographs in Geoffrey Godden's book on Caughley.

(9) 'Image' or 'Mother and Child' pattern shows a seated mother with a standing child on the right and a vase of fruit on the left. A secondary print usually shows a tall vase and a pedestal, with a protruding ladle handle and a kettle. The Caughley main print is similar to the Worcester one but the secondary prints are very different. The sequence of objects on the Worcester print, from left to right, are a tall vase of flowers, a tall pedestal, a large jar with ladle handle protruding, and a tea kettle; the Caughley version has a wide vase or jardinière of flowers, a bottle-shaped vase-like object, and a pot of flowers on a tripod-based stand.

(10) 'Parrot and Fruit' pattern, found on large objects such as mugs and jugs but not on tea ware. The best way of recognising the difference between the two versions is to note that the shading in the Worcester print is achieved by cross-hatching, particularly noticeable in the shaded rocks in the central foreground, whereas the Caughley version shows only straight or curved parallel lines of shading.

(11) 'Fence' pattern. The two versions are very similar, and so many re-engravings seem to have been done at each factory that it is hard to show consistency. It is best to look at the mass of rock shaped like a cornucopia, with trees growing from the top. The shading on the Worcester version is far heavier than on the Caughley and that of the rock on the right of the mass extends down to the ground, whereas on the Caughley it appears as a slight central shadow with an unshaded portion surrounding the shaded section.

(12) 'Three Flowers' was a very popular print showing three central flowers from which runs, to the right, a full-blown rose below two rose buds and, to the left, a downward-pointing convolvulus-type flower and leaves. The two versions are very similar indeed and one must rely on the different factory marks, or, if there are none, on the qualities of the material.

(13) 'La Pêche' and 'La Promenade Chinoise'. These two prints are usually found together. In the Worcester version of 'La Pêche' the fishing line tapers off from the rod in a continuous curve, whereas on the Caughley version the join between the tip of the rod and the line is quite distinct. In 'La Promenade Chinoise'—which shows a little boy going for a walk with his mother, who holds an open sunshade—the chin of the little boy is clear of his mother's skirt in the Worcester version, whereas in the Caughley the chin runs into the skirt. The trees to the left of the standing figure are smaller on the Worcester print than on the Caughley. A Worcester mug dated '1780' and a Caughley one dated '1790' show the relative lateness of this type.

(14) 'Birds in a Tree' is a very attractive scene showing birds—usually three, but sometimes two—in the branches of a tree, set in a landscape. There are a large number of variants from both factories, but the following are general variations. In the Worcester version, there are generally two birds flying in the sky; the hills in the background to the left of the tree are heavily shaded; and the centre hill has no dark patch at the top: the Caughley version normally has no birds flying in the sky; the hills are only slightly shaded; and the centre hill often shows a dark patch, as if it were a hollow volcano.

(15) 'Fruit and Wreath' shows a pumpkin type of fruit, with flowers and foliage set within oval or circular panels. Scattered small sprays are printed between the panels, and the whole is enclosed within an attractive looped-scroll border incorporating a running garland of flowers. In the Worcester version, the central fruit has much heavier shading and the two flowers in the lower-right-hand portion run into shaped portions of the fruit, whereas the same area on the

Caughley version is completely clear of shading, so that the two flowers which overlap the edge of the fruit at this point have a clear-cut outline.

From the above, and a careful study of the Caughley book by Geoffrey Godden, it should be a simple matter for the reader to sort out the basic differences between Worcester and Caughley, and it is hoped that these discoveries will cause a fresh look to be taken at ware which can be very charming. It must be said that not all Worcester of this period—especially that produced towards the end—is of great artistic merit; nor is all Caughley of poor quality. Far from it. There is just as much fine Caughley of this period as there is Worcester.

There are a number of characteristics of Worcester ware of this period, especially the blue printed pieces. The glaze is very bubbled, and this is particularly noticeable if examined through a magnifying glass. Glaze under the foot-rim often shows a considerable amount of black speckling. Foot-rings generally continue to show a glaze-free margin. The translucency of ware made up to about 1780 generally shows a green colour, varying from a pale yellow green to a much stronger green; but ware made after this date can just as frequently show a straw or pale orange colour. Nearer to 1790 this can be a much clearer whitish yellowy green. Printed ware often gives a heavily blued appearance, and many prints have areas of shading hand-painted in with a light wash—generally to indicate water, grass and shadows. Where gilding is used, it is always of the very highest Worcester quality—even when it consists of just a gilded line around the rim—and often gives a brighter appearance than the earlier softer brown colour.

It only remains to mention that no incised 'B' mark, usually thought to indicate a piece made after the arrival of Martin Barr in 1793, was found in any levels that would not be consistent with this idea. But a consideration of the ware made by Flight & Barr must wait for another volume. Likewise the ware of Chamberlain, throughout most of this period being bought in the white or already decorated from Flight and Caughley.

The great service made for the Duke of Clarence in 1792 (Plate 148) probably marked a water-shed, pointing the way to the great royal services to come. A plan of the site as it stood in 1793 (Plate 149) completes the story covered by this book.

Chapter IV

Checklist of Worcester Shapes

In this chapter, arranged in alphabetical order, are given different objects and vessels that are known to have been made at Worcester during the period covered by the book.

Not all the objects described were found on the site, but I am confident that the ascriptions are correct except where noted. Where sizes are reasonably consistent—as with moulded shapes—they are given, and this should provide a useful checklist for those wishing to compare their own pieces.

The uses to which some of the objects were put are not always very clear. It is unlikely that people in the eighteenth century used an object for only one purpose—a way of looking at shapes that is very much a modern one. Some of the Worcester objects obviously have a single definite use—such as teapots, coffee pots and chamber pots. But a number could have many uses—the objects called pickle trays, and roast-chestnut baskets. It is reasonable to suppose that a use could easily be found for a beautiful object, and what we generally refer to as pickle trays are merely referred to as 'leaves' in the price list quoted in Chapter I. The list should not be regarded as complete, as several other forms were undoubtedly made and may yet be discovered.

As an introduction to the checklist, there follows a note of the numbers of pieces and shapes that would be included in most standard dinner, dessert, tea and coffee services—although it must be realised that not all services were sold complete and the purchaser could have what he wanted.

Dinner Services

Worcester dinner services are not very common in the Dr. Wall period up to 1776. In the Davis/Flight period they are rarer still. Possibly, the difficulty of making large plates in the early period, and the comparable cheapness of the Chinese Nankin ware later, caused Worcester to concentrate more on the tea table than on the dinner table. A dinner service could contain one or more tureens; covers and stands of two sizes; a salad bowl; plates in different sizes

—probably up to 72; oblong dishes or meat platters; soup plates; and sauce-boats—possibly a pair.

Dessert Services

These varied greatly in make-up and many 'short' sets could be supplied. A specimen 'full' set in the 1769 catalogue contained forty-three pieces, made up as follows: three large round comports; four smaller round comports; four heart-shaped comports; four oval comports; two large round baskets; two cabbage leaves and twenty-four plates. A comport was simply a dessert dish, which could come in different shapes—square, heart-shaped, oval and two sizes of the round. Other items which could be included in dessert services were pierced baskets and stands, vine leaves and cream basins, covers and plates—the latter being sauce tureens, often now referred to as chestnut-baskets. The normal service had twenty-four plates.

By the 1780s, a fine 'full' service could have contained a centrepiece; a pair of ice pails, liners and covers; pairs of sugar and cream tureens, covers and stands with a pair of ladles; shell-shaped dishes; four melon-shaped dishes; four square dishes; four heart-shaped dishes; and twenty-four plates.

Tea Services

A complete tea and coffee service, on the basis of the 1769 catalogue, probably numbered forty-three pieces and consisted of a teapot and cover; coffee pot and cover; twelve teacups; twelve saucers; six coffee cups; a teapot stand; a bason plate (slop basin); a sugar dish (sucrier), cover and plate; a milk pot (milk jug); a spoon boat (spoon tray); tea-jar and cover (teapoy) and a cream ewer.

By the 1780s the usual make-up of a service was a teapot and cover and stand; a spoon tray; a tea canister and cover; a sugar bowl and cover; a slop bowl; two bread and butter plates of different sizes; twelve tea bowls; twelve handled coffee cups; and twelve saucers. By this time, it was unusual to have a coffee pot in the service and some 'short' services only had eight cups and saucers.

THE OBJECTS

Asparagus Servers

Asparagus servers have a fan-shaped flat base, the wide end curved and the narrow end straight, both ends with rounded edges, and two side pieces of curving shape with a raised projection in the middle. They are usually painted with a cell border at the wider fan shaped end and flowers of the tulip variety on the flat base, with straight lines and a curved and dotted border—similar to border number 24—at the narrow end. A number of these objects which are often ascribed to Worcester may well be Derby. The Caughley factory made many examples, mostly decorated with the 'Fisherman' pattern.

Overall length, 3 inches; width, $1\frac{7}{10}$ inches widening to $2\frac{7}{10}$ inches.

Found in disturbed levels on the site.

Baskets

Pierced open baskets, or those having a cover and stand, exist in many versions. Oval and round ones, the latter pierced with fourteen interlacing circles joined by straps, are often decorated with coloured grounds and flowers and date from about 1760. Larger, more elaborate baskets, with moulded panels on the body which can be pierced or not, usually have elaborately hand-modelled flowers and leaves applied at each end of the basket and have a stand and cover, both of which are pierced (Plate 122). Some of them have embossed mark 'T°' on the base, near the foot-ring. The baskets and covers are often simply decorated in underglaze blue, but some are beautifully decorated in a wide palette of onglaze colours (Colour Plate VII). They would seem to date from about 1768 and run on into the Davis/ Flight period, with the baskets more simply decorated with just gold lines. More simple baskets with modelled flowers are found marked with 'Flight' in script and with a small crescent (Plate 143).

Length varies.

Found on the site in most levels from 1 to 6.

Bell Pulls (or Curtain Pulls)

Only one of these interesting objects has been seen by me. It is of egg-shape, with a small round hole at the top and a larger one at the bottom, beautifully decorated in Oriental style with bands of underglaze blue alternating with bands of onglaze Oriental flowers and gilding. From the material and decoration, it is certainly Worcester of about 1775–95. These objects were made by both Flight and Chamberlain.

Length, 2 inches.

Not found on the site.

Billing Doves/Tureen

A pair of billing doves forming a tureen is believed to be Worcester and is very rare.

Bleeding Bowls

Bleeding bowls—or they might be porringers—are round bowls with a rounded rim and one elaborately scroll-moulded handle.

Diameter, $5\frac{1}{4}$ inches. From about 1753 or so.

Not found on site.

Bonbonniers

Believed to be Worcester; a circular box with concave sides and slightly convex lid, hinged with a brass mount.

Diameter, $2\frac{3}{4}$ inches.

Not found on site.

Bough Pots (or Crocus Pots)

There are two main forms of these objects, which may either have been for growing crocus bulbs in—the flowers emerging through the different sized holes—or for arranging leaves and flowers. Like cornucopias, they sometimes have two pierced holes in their flat backs for affixing to a wall.

The most common version is shown in Plate 78 and is of *Bombe* form with shell and rococo moulded borders. Most of these have scale blue decoration with fabulous birds, as in the illustration; but others have underglaze printed sprays or birds of an unusual Bristol/Worcester type in onglaze decoration— so presumably the vessels could date from before 1760.

Height, $5\frac{1}{2}$ inches; length, $8\frac{1}{2}$ inches; width, 5 inches.

The other version is of 'D' shape with a frilled edge of twelve indentations or flutes at the front and five flutes at the rear; generally decorated only in onglaze colours.

Height, $5\frac{5}{8}$ inches; length, 8 inches; width, $7\frac{3}{4}$ inches.

Not found on the site.

BOWLS—see Slop Bowls

Broth Bowls

Two-handled bowls with a small cover, of rather late period. The handles are set close to a rise above the rounded rim of the bowl. Generally printed with florals and painted cell borders.

Diameter across handles, $7\frac{1}{4}$ inches.

Butter Coolers

So-called butter coolers are oval vessels standing on feet, the body pierced all over with circular holes, even the base; a domed cover has a knob of an apple and two leaves.

Length, 5½ inches; width, 4½ inches.

A fragment was found on the site in a disturbed level, but probably dating from the 1770s.

Butter Pots, Tubs or Tureens

These exist in two forms—circular and oval. The former should stand on a circular stand and have thin, rather flat, applied leaves; the latter should have an oval stand and cover. Both are usually decorated with underglaze printing or painting and are probably of post-1770 date. Similar shapes were made at Caughley and at Lowestoft, the potting of these copies being generally coarser and with much thicker applied leaves than those of the Worcester originals. (See Geoffrey Godden's books on the Caughley and the Lowestoft porcelain.)

Found on the site from Pit 1 onwards.

Buttons

These were one of the surprises of the excavation. Three different sizes are shown in Plate 147. The smallest size was found merely in the white, probably intended for onglaze decoration; the larger sizes were decorated with circles of underglaze blue, which suggest some form of gilding or onglaze colours, although some were completely coloured in blue. They each have a loop on the back for attachment to the clothing, but these were all broken on the site wasters. It would be most interesting to learn if there is anyone with knowledge of eighteenth century clothing having similar buttons. Dated about 1785 to 1790, the buttons were found on the site at Level 3 associated with 'willow' patterns of the late Davis/Flight period. Similar buttons were found on the Caughley site.

Diameter, 1 to 1¼ inches.

Cabaret

These, believed to be Worcester, are very rare. They consist of a large tray of irregular oval shape with a wavy edge having eight indentations. They have two wells of 2½ inches diameter at either end and two smaller ones in between which hold a teapot of barrel shape, a sucrier, a milk jug and a cup and saucer.

Candlesticks (Hand)

These are not very common, and only one was found on the site. Plate 97 gives a good impression of a hand candlestick which has a round shallow dish, an embossed flattened rim, and an embossed centre from which stands the candle holder. Sometimes the rim is pierced. The double curved handle emerges from a man's face mask at the rim. The foot is turned and has a pierced hole running into the centre of the candle holder, set a little off centre. Painted generally with late looking daffodil-type and other flowers under-glaze, although coloured versions are known. Also known from Caughley.

Diameter, $5\frac{3}{5}$ inches; height, $2\frac{1}{10}$ inches.

Found on the site in Pit 1. Circa 1770 onwards.

Candlesticks (Table or Pillar)

These are very rare and are found in two forms, one type having a circular mound base with gadroon moulding around it, and a stem rising to a moulded gadroon knop which supports the base of the nozzle, topped by similar moulding. Decorated underglaze with flower sprays.

Height, $9\frac{1}{2}$ inches; diameter at base, 5 inches.

The other type is of silver shape with baluster columns and a squared moulded base.

One of the figures of the 'Gardener' is formed as a candlestick; see under Figures.

Caudle Cups and Chocolate Cups

There is considerable confusion over the differences between these two objects. It is possible that chocolate cups were not meant to have covers and often had a wavy top, whereas caudle cups probably had covers—Chamberlain's order books contain frequent references like '4 Caudle cups and covers, Royal stripe'—and were taller and narrower than chocolate cups. They are both of ogee shape, generally with two handles but sometimes with one, the handles often ending in duck-head terminals (Plate 74).

Found on the site in Level 5.

Cauliflower Tureens

These tureens, in the form of a cauliflower, are scarce. They should have a stand in the form of a cauliflower leaf, and the decoration on both tureen and stand is of onglaze printed butterflies, more rarely coloured in. The shape is based upon Chelsea examples, as are the partridge (or quail) tureens, and they probably date from about 1765 or so (Plate 35).

Length of dish, 8¼ inches; height of tureen and cover, 3 inches; width, 4 inches.

Not found on site.

Chamber Pots

These are very rare objects indeed, although it is rather surprising as several fragments were found on the site and quantities must have been made. Possibly being a very utilitarian object they would tend to get broken and then thrown away. Plate 44 shows the shape of one which is printed underglaze with floral sprays and with painted cell border.

6⅝ inches diameter. From about 1765.

Chocolate Cups—see Caudle Cups

Coffee Pots

These, like teapots, are invariably of excellent design and potting. They vary enormously in size and were included in the normal tea and coffee services made at most factories. A number are illustrated in this book. One common characteristic is that the cover often has a large overhang to the rim, making it appear a size too large for its body. The underneath part of the flange of the cover has the glaze cleaned off.

Coffee pots can be of thrown shape but are just as frequently of various moulded forms. Common forms are feather moulding and straight flutes, and they can be found with most of the patterns—both under- and onglaze, printed and painted—that are used for services. A particularly beautiful one is shown in Colour Plate VIII, decorated with a pattern of the late 1770s. Later coffee pots, of the 1780s, can have a flat button-shape knob (Plate 140).

Cornucopias

These objects, in the shape of Roman cornucopias, were presumably made as pairs, as the narrow rounded ends curl in opposite ways to complement each other. There are two basic forms, one having a spirally ribbed pattern with underglaze painted flowering branches below a band of embossed flowers, and the other having a much more elaborate modelled rural landscape scene with a church at the top, a man seated below a tree, two cows, cottages, and flowering trees and plants. Both forms are flat-backed, with two suspension holes pierced through the back at the top, intended for suspension on a wall for flower arrangement.

Height, 8½ inches. Circa 1755.

Found in Level 7, and modelling of the elaborate cornucopia is very similar to the cream-boat shown in Plate 5.

Cream-Boats

Cream-boats were made throughout the whole of the period covered by this book and are to be seen in a number of the illustrations. They differ from milk jugs in that the jugs stand upright.

Moulded cream-boats of the 1770s and later can often be confused with those of Caughley, but the Worcester ones are wider in the body—2⅔ inches at the top, as against the $2\frac{1}{10}$ inches of Caughley. Other differences may be seen in the comparative photographs in Geoffrey Godden's Caughley book.

A wide range of patterns may be found, both under and onglaze.

Cress Dishes

Cress dishes should have a stand to catch the water which drains through the pierced holes in the well of the dish. They are of relatively late date and are generally decorated with underglaze printed floral sprays. It is very doubtful whether Caughley made any, and they are rare in Worcester.

Crocus Pots—see Bough Pots

Cups and Saucers

These vary from the early Bristol/Worcester tea bowls (Plate 8) and cups with elaborate handles (Plate 15) to the plainer tea bowls and cups of the Dr. Wall and the Davis/Flight periods. Handles are usually of a ribbed loop shape; the nicely turned foot-rings are generally of triangular shape, with no glaze on the bottom of the foot-rim and often with a pegged glaze-free margin on the base just inside the foot-rim. The rims, particularly of the bowls, are usually chamfered on the outside, and the bodies are generally turned thin. In the Davis/Flight period, the saucers become a little deeper in shape and a new shape of cup with a curved body slightly resembling an ogee shape—as seen on the chocolate cups—is seen, associated particularly with the 'blue lily' pattern and the simple underglaze 'blue diamond' patterns (Plate 144).

Custard Cups

Cups with a bulbous body, everted lip and, generally, the curious peaked handle shown in Plate 52 are often referred to as custard cups. They seem to run through the whole of the 1760s and are often decorated with Oriental onglaze patterns. They should have a cover, generally with a flower finial.

From $2\frac{1}{4}$ inches in height.

Decanters

Vases of decanter shape are rare. One of these is encrusted with applied floral swags and ribbon bows, painted in between with dry-blue sprays.

Height, 7 inches. Circa 1770–75.

Not found on the site.

Dishes

Large dishes from the earliest period are known: of elaborately rococo-scroll modelled edges, including lizards, birds, fish and insects among the decoration, $18\frac{1}{2}$ inches in length; of octagonal, straight-sided shape, approximately 13 inches in length—found in the lowest levels—painted underglaze with flowering rocks and fence (see Watney's *English Blue and White Porcelain*, plate 28B) which dates from about 1755 and is rare.

Elaborate dishes of irregular oval shape moulded with strapwork, vine leaves and tendrils were found in Pits 4 and 3 and would date from about 1760 to 1768 (Plate 41). They are decorated with underglaze floral prints; others can be decorated with onglaze colours or with ground colours. Different sized dishes of oval and octagonal shape are parts of services dating from about 1768 onwards, generally decorated with 'blue sprays' underglaze prints and painted borders (border number 18). Beautiful irregularly oval dishes with wavy rims, moulded with rococo scrolls, are pierced with four panels of trellis work, moulded basket work panels in between these—$10\frac{2}{5}$ inches long and $8\frac{9}{10}$ inches wide. Large oval-shaped dishes with a wavy edge (Plate 69), $11\frac{1}{4}$ inches long, probably date from after 1760. Kidney-shaped dishes, from dessert services, are of various sizes and do not have any modelling.

The most elaborate dishes made at Worcester are of diamond shape with moulded shells in the four corners of the wide rim, which has extremely fine piercing, $15\frac{1}{4}$ inches long and $11\frac{3}{4}$ inches wide. These can have decoration varying from turquoise borders and Oriental style flowers to simple gilding, and they seem to run from the 1760s to the 1770s (Plate 62).

Dishes of irregular square shape with twelve indentations generally carry a blue border of the 1770s.

Egg Cups

Egg cups naturally vary slightly in size as they were hand-thrown pieces. Plate 92 shows two different forms that were found on the site—one of the normal plain shape and one with groups of simple embossed flowers. The latter is a form not known to me as a finished piece and should well repay looking for. The bases can be either flat or slightly hollowed, sometimes partly glazed underfoot; and they are generally decorated underglaze with simple painted flower sprays, with cell or a more elaborate diaper and lozenge border.

Egg Drainers

These are large caddy-type spoons with pierced holes in the base of the bowl for draining the eggs while being removed from the boiling water. They are usually decorated with underglaze blue floral sprays.

Found on the site in disturbed levels.

Eye Baths

These vary slightly in size and actual form, having a boat-shaped top and a narrow stem, sometimes with a bulbous knop and a hollow foot. An unusual form found on the site is shown in Plate 147. The usual decoration is underglaze painted flower sprays with a cell border. Probably of the 1770s.

Height, about 2 inches.

Figures

It was long assumed that Worcester made no figures; but there are contemporary references to Worcester figures, and many attempts have been made to discover them by such means as analysis of the body and comparisons of the modelled flowers that were put on some. By these methods, the following figures have become accepted as Worcester.

1. A pair of a Turk and his companion (see Colour Plate VI), the former with his left hand on his sword and right hand on his hip, the latter with his left hand on his hip. They stand on small bun bases, with small flowers at their feet; some of the flower buds have hot-cross-bun strokes, as if the bud were just about to burst. Height from about 5 to $5\frac{1}{2}$ inches.

2. A pair of a gardener and his female companion, the former holding a pot of flowers in his right hand and his left hand resting on a spade, the latter carrying a posy of flowers in her right hand and a basket of flowers over her left arm. They are also on bun bases, with similar flowers and buds. About $6\frac{1}{2}$ inches high.

3. A pair of a sportsman and his female companion. He wears a frock coat. His right hand holds the muzzle of a musket, the butt of which rests on the ground, and his left hand is behind his back. His companion has a flowered hat and carries a powder flask. They stand on moulded bases with a small shell thumb-piece at the front. A mass of May blossom grows up each side of the figures.

4. 'La Nourrice': a nurse, seated on a low pedestal, bending over a swaddled child lying on her lap, the baby's right hand held up to the nurse's right breast. This is about $5\frac{9}{10}$ inches high as against the Chelsea model from which it is copied, which is usually $7\frac{1}{2}$ inches high. This is now thought to be Liverpool (see *English Ceramic Circle Transactions*, Vol. 7, Part 1, 1968).

5. A bird of the kingfisher type, found in the white with gilding, one form having a fish lying in front of it on the modelled tree-stump-like base, with modelled flowers which include hot-cross-bun type buds. $5\frac{1}{4}$ inches from tail to beak. These are now thought to be from Chamberlain's factory.

6. A group of two canaries on sprays of apple blossom, on modelled base with shell thumb piece at the front and a handle at the rear similar to ones on baskets. A number of the flower buds show hot-cross-bun crosses (Colour Plate VI).

While no fragments of any of these were found on the site, without evidence to the contrary it must be assumed that they are of Worcester make and were being made by 1771 when both Mrs. Powys and Captain Roche report having seen figures being made. They could well have started under the influence of the modeller who used the mark 'T°' and similar variants, for the hot-cross-bun buds and the flower modelling are very similar to those on a large basket in the Dyson Perrins Collection having an embossed 'T°' mark on the base.

The model of one positive Worcester figure was, however, found: a figure group of Cupid at Vulcan's forge, which has always been thought of as from Longton Hall and is so ascribed in *English Porcelain 1745-1850*, Ernest Benn Ltd., 1965, Plate 23A. The pitcher model found on the site positively identifies this group as Worcester, the slightly larger size accounted for by a reduction of about a sixth in the size of the finished piece during the biscuit firing. Although the model was found in Level 3, there had been some disturbance of the ground by the building of the river wall. It is therefore rather difficult to place a close date upon the figure, but the style could well place it in the 1760s. That a number of other Worcester figures of the years around 1770 must exist there can be little doubt, and the continuing search for them will undoubtedly occupy collectors for years to come. The small cow on top of the pot shown in Plate 49 is yet another indication that Worcester was capable of making such things; and there is also the possibility that a small sheep on a rock base may be a product of the factory—but the author has not seen this piece. It is possible that when the landscaped gardens that will lie across part of the Warmstry House site are being bulldozed some fragments may be found. A very careful watch will be kept.

Finger Bowls and Stands

The bowls have a waisted cylindrical shape and either a wavy edge, shown in Plate 20, or a round edge as in Plate 31. The latter is possibly the earlier shape, appearing generally with early onglaze prints of birds. The wavy-edged shape was found on the site in circumstances which suggest it is later than the other type, and the decorations are often in onglaze colours. The fragment shown, however, is of an early blue and white pattern of the 'Cormorant'.

Flowerpots

Large flowerpots—as shown in Colour Plate I, of hexagonal shape, with a circular hole in the base and having a low hexagonal stand—are known. Flower-tubs are known—tub-like pots with a flanged mouth and two moulded horizontal bands, from the upper of which depend three moulded gilt rings, evenly spaced, with a conical encrusted floral bouquet composed of garden flowers growing out of the pot. The latter shape is similar to the fragment of waster shown in Plate 147, and a typical one is about $5\frac{1}{2}$ inches in height. Circa 1770–75.

Hors D'Œuvres Sets

Small flat-bottomed dishes of lobed shape, a short one-fluted side widening out into a fan shape. The short side is made to fit into a star-shaped centre which is surrounded by six of the dishes fitting into each other. The difficulty of making these little objects was very great as all the component parts had to fit into each other after firing. It was important, therefore, that no distortion should take place; and some examples of firing supports were found on the site. Also found was a large part of the centre, clearly shown in Plate 93, which is rare. Dishes are decorated underglaze, usually with a bird perched on a flowering rock.

Length of dishes, about $2\frac{3}{4}$ inches; diameter of centre piece, approximately $3\frac{1}{2}$ inches across points, $1\frac{9}{10}$ inches across the base; height $1\frac{1}{8}$ inches. From about 1755 to 1760.

Ice Pails

Ice pails are of tub shape with two shell handles, and they should have a bowl-shape inner liner and a cover with sunken central handle. The usual type of decoration has underglaze blue borders and various forms of onglaze colours and gilding.

8 inches by 8 inches. From about 1770.

Not found on the site.

Ink Pots

These are usually nearly cylindrical, with spreading base, having four pen-holes on the shoulder and a cup-shape mouthed detachable well. Usually decorated in onglaze colours, but sometimes with underglaze blue flowers of a late date.

Diameter, $5\frac{3}{4}$ inches; height, $3\frac{1}{4}$ inches. From about 1770.

Not found on the site.

Jugs

These vessels vary in size from small milk jugs to great mask jugs. Most of the earliest jugs were based on silver shapes, the first non-silver forms being the ring-necked mask-spout large jugs and the smaller sparrow-beak milk jugs.

Cream jugs of pear shape, with large inset lip higher than the rear part of the rim, and with a handle similar to the cup in Plate 52 vary from 3 to $3\frac{1}{2}$ inches in height. Sparrow-beak jugs—the lips resembling the perky beak of a sparrow—vary from 3 to 6 inches in height and generally have loop handles. Cream jugs of elaborate moulded form with a scalloped-shell design and a handle in the form of a lamprey are 3 inches high to the top of the handle and $3\frac{1}{2}$ inches long.

Barrel-shaped jugs with moulded lines which vary somewhat and moulded floral and leaf decoration on the body are an attractive shape (Plate 105). Larger jugs are either of the round-necked type (Plate 26) or the mask-lip type (Plate 28), the latter probably overlapping the former but continuing right to the end of the Davis/Flight period. There are two main forms of the mask: the simple one which can be seen in Plate 42, and an early, more elaborate, form with a sort of crown above the mask.

An early water jug and basin is found (Plate 21).

Junket and Salad Dishes

These large dishes were found in considerable variety on the site—a great number in Pit 4—and three examples are shown in Plate 95. They have shaped edges with various mouldings below, such as six scallop shells. In the centre is a six-petalled flower similar to a Tudor rose. The diameter of the dishes is generally just over 9 inches.

Another popular form has an octofoil lobed border and a centre formed of overlapping leaves with a central medallion. The diameter is $10\frac{1}{2}$ inches. This form is usually decorated in onglaze colours, whereas the others can often be decorated in underglaze blue, as shown in the illustration.

Knife and Fork Handles

A number of different forms of these were found on the site, from straight rounded handles of plain form, and also with modelling resembling chrysanthemums, to pistol-grip forms. Most of those found were decorated with simple floral sprays, but one fragment was of a 'Queen Charlotte' pattern decorated handle. Scale blue and onglaze decorated handles are known but were not found on the site. Some typical fragments are shown in Plate 89.

Ladles

Large sauce ladles are found in a number of versions, the handle generally having a nicely curved shape. The bowl can either be round or have a wavy edge. A typical one is $6\frac{1}{2}$ inches long, the bowl 2 inches in diameter; and the handle ends in a shell-like scroll under the base.

Leaf Dishes

Leaf dishes exist in a number of different forms ranging from very small leaves with the end of the stalk as a handle (Plate 109), modelled veining underneath, to much more elaborate leaves with modelled veins inside the leaf and applied twig handle. Large dishes formed of two overlapping leaves with raised veins are $13\frac{1}{2}$ inches long and $9\frac{3}{4}$ inches wide (Plate 45); these are often decorated with underglaze prints. Oval dishes having twenty indentations with moulded intersecting semicircles below, and at either end a vine-leaf spray forming a twig handle, usually have ground and onglaze colours. Some of these were found on the site decorated with underglaze floral prints (Plate 41). Dishes of cabbage-leaf form, the stalk handle being carried round as the mid-rib, are $8\frac{1}{2}$ inches long.

Most of these shapes are from about 1760.

Mugs and Tankards

These have so many variants that only the principal forms will be mentioned. The early ones generally have swelling bases (Plate 6), later becoming either straight-sided (Plate 37) or bell-shaped (Plate 43)—the last seeming to drop out by 1770 but the straight-sided form continuing into the Davis/Flight period. Handles are generally of ribbed strap shape, and the mugs are always turned to a very thin gauge—much thinner than Caughley ones, for example. Most Worcester mugs—from about 1760, at any rate—have rims which are chamfered slightly on the outside, a very characteristic effect which is so different from the curved rim of Caughley mugs. The sizes of these mugs vary enormously, from very small ones of only 3 inches in height to large ones of 6 inches in height.

G

Mustard Pots

Two types of mustard pot are known. Wet-mustard pots are straight-sided with a straight narrow neck and flattish cover, with sometimes a hole for a spoon. A dry-mustard pot has an elongated pear-shaped body with a high-domed cover surmounted by a conical knob (Plate 67). Both types also occur in Caughley versions.

Partridge Tureens

These, like the cauliflower tureens, are rare in Worcester. They are in the form of a partridge sitting on its nest, the top part of the bird lifting off (Plate 114), and were probably copied from Chelsea originals. The price list quoted in Chapter 1 refers to two sizes at a cost of 7/– and 8/– each, fully enamelled; but only the one size has been found. Likely to be from the mid 1760s.

Length varies from 6 to 6½ inches; height, 4 to 5 inches, with head.

Patty Pans or Tart Pans

Worcester patty pans are round with a flat edge. Decoration is only found in blue and white.

Height, 2½ inches; diameter, 4¾ inches.

Pipe Bowl

This, believed to be a Worcester object, has a two-part bowl with mounts, chain and hinged perforated lid of brass. The lower part of the bowl is moulded in the form of a coiled fish, from the open mouth of which issues the base of the stem.

Height, 4 inches; width, 2½ inches.

Not found on the site.

Pipe Stopper

One is known: the head and shoulders of the 'gardener's companion' figure but with a ribbon at the neck.

Plates

Early plates are not very common. Heavy round plates with a wide flange, painted underglaze 'flowering rocks' and 'fence' patterns or 'Long Elizas', sometimes have a Chinese 'precious objects' mark underneath. Diameter, 9 inches.

Later Worcester plates of the 1760s typically have a rim with twenty-four fluted indentations, as in Plate 73, or with twelve nicked indentations and also a round shape.

Soup plates generally have a plain round rim. Shallow, curving, bowl-like plates are usually termed cake plates. Plate rims with pierced edges are very rare.

Pots of Flowers—see Flower Pots

Punch Bowls

Large thrown bowls, often with a hunting scene painted onglaze, are frequently met with and are splendid objects—the only weak point being that the punch, or the action of the ladle, affected the print inside the bowl and it is common to find this print rather badly worn (Plate 38).

Punch Kettles

Occasionally, very large teapots are seen—rarely, with a figure of a running fox and the words 'Tally, Ho' beneath the spout.

Height, 9 inches with conical knob; diameter, 6 inches.

Rice Bowls

Round bowls on a foot, the cover of high-domed shape—usually with flower knob and a square hole at the rim of the cover for the spoon. The cover is pierced with a pattern of holes resembling grains of rice, with other patterned groups of pierced holes, including heart shapes, below. A painted border rather similar to No. 18.

Diameter, $5\frac{1}{2}$ inches.

Not found on the site.

Salts

A standing or master salt having four napkin rests on the top is known, 4 inches in diameter, and Chelsea-type salts of a shell standing on a base of encrusted shells and corals, similar to the sweetmeat dishes. A more normal looking form of salt-cellar is in the Perrins Museum but is very rare.

Not found on the site.

Salad Bowls (see Junket Dishes)

Sauce-Boats

These vary enormously throughout the period and a number of illustrations are shown in the book. The types shown in the group of Bristol marked pieces (Plate 2) continued into the Dr. Wall period, although the elaborate, high double-scrolled handles were soon simplified—probably because the high, top loop was easily broken. Boats modelled on silver shapes continued into the mid 1750s, one version being two-handled with a lobed lip at each end. Some of the handles have knobs in the shape of a monkey's head. A type formed of moulded cos lettuce leaves with a lip curving to the left for right-handed pouring, which was disputed for a long time, was found on the site in the 1978 excavations and is now undoubtedly Worcester, two different sizes being made.

Shell Dishes

These range from small shells of scallop form, $3\frac{2}{5}$ inches long and $3\frac{1}{5}$ inches wide, to a shell with plain scalloped edge, $5\frac{1}{10}$ inches long and $4\frac{3}{5}$ inches wide.

Slop Bowls

Large bowls were probably used for slops but undoubtedly could have had a number of other uses. Worcester thrown bowls always exhibit superb potting techniques with body walls of even thickness throughout and generally with nicely turned foot-rings and chamfered rims. (Also see Punch Bowls.)

Spittoons

Globular bowls with wide, everted lips are referred to as spittoons, although they might have actually been used as bulb pots and are sometimes called flower vases today. Caughley versions also occur.

Height, 4 inches; diameter at rim, 5 inches.

Not found on the site, but late—probably of 1770s and after.

Spoons

A group of spoons found on the site is shown in Plate 89. The one with the frilled, shell-like end is very rare.

Spoon Trays

These flat-based objects exist in a large number of forms. A variety can be seen in H. Rissik Marshall's *Coloured Worcester Porcelain*, Plate 26, all the forms shown being found on the site at levels ranging from about 1760 to 1780. One form with eight lobes has floral moulding inside; the others have no moulding. Most are of hexagonal oblong shape with lobes and vary from 5 to $6\frac{3}{4}$ inches in length and $2\frac{2}{3}$ to $3\frac{1}{2}$ inches in width.

Strainers

Circular with one applied branch handle, these are pierced in the base with a number of holes usually arranged in a regular pattern. Worcester examples are rare, Caughley examples being relatively common.
   Diameter, $3\frac{1}{8}$ inches.
   Not found on the site.

Sucriers

Sucriers are rather like tall bowls with a high cover, often having a double curve, which sits upon the bowl by a flange (Plate 117).

Sundial

The Perrins Museum has an interesting sundial, the details being painted and bearing the name of Josiah Holdship, one of the fifteen original partners. No other examples are known.

Table Centres or Sweetmeat Dishes

These great groups of dishes piled up on mounds of moulded shells are generally referred to as sweetmeat dishes. A typical one is shown in Plate 123 —but they could be much more complicated, with ten dishes and rising to $10\frac{1}{2}$ inches in height. Decoration can vary from blue and white, and natural painted shells, to the simplest of gold borders. The shapes probably date from the period of the 'T^{o}' mark—late 1760s into the 1780s.

Teapots

Teapots are among the finest objects produced by Worcester, and a number of typical shapes are shown in the illustrations in this book. Those of the

Bristol/Worcester period are often of silver shape; and the usual Dr. Wall period ones are of round shape, typically having an ear-like handle of round form or with a double ridge on top and a nicely curved spout rising as high as or just higher than the rim—a knob in the form of a flower being more common than a pointed cone, the under-flange of the cover being cleared of glaze, and the body of the pot having from four to eight pierced strainer holes. This form of pot continued into the Davis/Flight period; but a number of other shapes were also used in the 1760s and early 1770s, such as barrel and bullet shapes—to be followed by oval shapes.

Covers of the late 1770s and 1780s are often flatter in form and fit nearly flush with the rim, the later versions generally having flat, button knobs.

Ribbed teapots of this late period have twenty-four convex ribs as against the thirty on the similar Caughley shape.

Teapot Stands

A teapot should generally have a stand, of a shape suiting that of the teapot. The stands always have a flat base, unglazed underneath.

Tea Caddies and Canisters

The typical Dr. Wall period caddy shape has an ovoid body, slight foot and straight narrow neck, and is topped by a small cover with flower knob (Plate 76). It can have decoration ranging from the simple blue and white to the finest grounds and onglaze decoration, depending on the service it accompanies. From the early 1770s the shape becomes of canister form, widening upwards to a sloping shoulder and with a flattish cover—first with a flower knob and then with a flat button-shape knob (Plate 126).

Larger tea canisters which swell out rather more bulbously to the shoulder of 5-inch height and $3\frac{1}{4}$-inch diameter at the top and $2\frac{1}{4}$-inch at the bottom are known, marked with two forms of tea—'Bohea' and 'Green'. But these are rare and were not found on the site.

Tokens

Very rare small circular flat tokens exist which were issued by the Company, probably to its workers, at a time of shortage of small coinage of the realm. They are in two sizes—for 1/- and 2/- with a moulded mark 'WPC' (Worcester Porcelain Company) on their backs and onglaze printed inscription on the front directing that they may be redeemed at the Porcelain Manufactory and signed 'W. Davis'. A full set may be seen at the Dyson Perrins Museum (Plate 127).

Tumblers

These are rare in the Dr. Wall period, two known examples having green grounds and onglaze flowers. In the Davis/Flight period a number were produced, and a typical example is shown in Plate 145.

Tureens

Apart from tureens in the shape of different objects, and the large early ones as shown in Plate 18, two main types were made: small ones of oval shape, the edge having four indentations, 6¾ inches long and 4 inches wide, with a stand, cover and ladle, the knob often in the form of an artichoke bud and two leaves; and larger ones of the type shown from the Duke of Gloucester service in Colour Plate IV, which is about 9¼ inches long, with shell shape handles. Some covers have an elaborate knob in the form of acorns and oak leaves.

Vases

There are so many different forms of vase that it would take a whole book to describe them all. They range from the curious, frequently hexagonal vases of Bristol/Worcester type to the very large vases of the Dr. Wall period; from simple thrown shapes to hexagonally moulded shapes; from large thrown vases with applied rococo scroll handles to elaborate pieces of Chelsea type with pierced panels and masses of applied flowers. Other forms are of classical urn shape with two upward standing handles of scroll form, small mouth and a domed cover, with coloured decoration or simple underglaze blue, from about 1770; vases imitating Chinese bronze vessels of large size, 16 inches high; small wide-mouthed vases with a bulge near the bottom (Plate 50); and goblet-shaped vases with pierced rim (Plate 82).

Water Bottles and Basins

There are two main types of water bottle: a thrown shape shown in Plate 17; and an octagonal shape with bulbous body, long neck and a bulge an inch below the neck. The latter would be later than the thrown form, often with powder-blue ground and onglaze colours—basin, 4 inches high and 11 inches diameter; bottle, 10 inches high.

Wine Funnels

Funnels can be decorated in blue and white or with onglaze Chinoiserie. They are very rare.

Height, 5 inches; diameter at mouth, 5 inches.

Not found on the site.

Wine Tasters

Pretty little objects in the shape of a half peach, with a twig handle set at the side. They are very rare.

Height, $1\frac{1}{2}$ inches; diameter, 4 inches.

Not found on the site, but about 1760 in date.

Chapter V

Identifying Worcester—Marks and Fakes

One of the most frequent questions asked by visitors to the Dyson Perrins Museum is, 'How can we identify Worcester of the eighteenth century?' The desire is for an easy set of rules that can be applied to decide where and when the piece was made, in the same way that the hall-marks on silver can be used.

Unfortunately, there is no easy set of rules; no ready reckoner with which to add up a number of clues and produce the answer. There are too many variables in early porcelain—so many differences that can occur between one kiln firing and another, between one workman and another, or by the same workman at different times.

The usual methods given in most books for recognising Worcester of the pre-Flight & Barr periods can be summarised as follows: all ware show a green translucency by holding them up to a standard electric light bulb of about 100 watts; all foot-rings are of nicely triangular shape; the insides of foot-rings always show a wiped away glaze-free margin; no Worcester glaze is ever crazed.

Those who have read the book to this point will have realised that most of these points are no longer valid.

Some of them, however, can still be held as general features of Worcester: no crazing of the glaze is ever found, and the ware is generally of good taste and of fine quality. But these two points can be held for some other English porcelain factories. The other points are too variable to be relied upon for certainty.

How, then, can one hope to build up a sure confidence in recognising Worcester?

I would suggest that the following points offer the most satisfactory way:

1. Close examination of the moulded shapes and patterns outlined and illustrated in this book, which can be taken as being certain Worcester ones.
2. Frequent handling of positive Worcester material, either at the view days of good auction sales or at antique shops.

3. Frequent visits to the major collections of Worcester porcelain, a list of which are given in the Bibliography.

Handling of the material is the surest way to a greater understanding, and I would suggest that the collector tries to build up as large a collection as possible of standard Worcester shapes and patterns. This can be done for a reasonable outlay providing he is not greatly worried about the condition of the pieces and is prepared to accept damaged pieces—even badly damaged ones. The latter are extremely useful for gaining the essential *feel* of Worcester. A bowl with a great chip out of the rim can train the senses as well as, if not better than, a perfect piece; for instance, it is possible to examine the granular structure of the body from such a damaged piece.

The first essential thing for a collector to have clear in his mind is the difference between the soft paste porcelain which was the product of most of the English factories from the mid to late eighteenth century, the hard paste porcelain of Europe and the true porcelain of the Orient. This basic knowledge of the difference between the main types of early porcelain is so essential that the new collector should not dream of starting collecting until he has mastered it. Most antique dealers will be only too delighted to spare the time it takes to demonstrate and once the differences in feel and look are realised the beginner is well on the road to greater understanding.

A basic knowledge of the different bodies will save numerous heartbreaks caused by buying Chinese blue and white porcelain in the belief that it is the so different soft paste English material, or relatively modern French hard paste copies, or fakes of scale blue Worcester.

No amount of words or photographs can show the difference between the glassy, hard, cold qualities of hard paste porcelain and the granular, softer, warmer effect of the English soft paste ware. This can be appreciated very easily by handling.

It is very much more difficult to differentiate between the ware of the various English factories making soft paste porcelain, but building up a collection of small pieces from each of the main factories will help enormously. This might be done by, say, a collection of teacups—one of each of the different factories—which would show the difference between the bone-ash body of, for instance, Bow and the more compact soapstone body of Worcester.

As to deciding whether a piece is Worcester, although most of the old methods of recognition have now to be viewed with suspicion it is possible to use them to assist in a decision.

If the shape and size match up exactly with the details in this book, the piece can be taken as authentic. If the exact shape is not shown here, look for the qualities expected—that is: generally good potting and decoration; translucency generally of a green colour, varying from a strong green in the early years to a yellow green around the end of the Dr. Wall period to a possible straw/orange in the late Davis/Flight period; foot-rims generally of wedge or triangular shape, although a number of undercut ones are to be found; feet generally wiped clear of glaze, as is the case with the flanges of covers; the inside of foot-rims of ware from about 1760 often showing signs of 'pegging'; the glaze always very well fitting and uncrazed, showing slight green pooling in the early days and frequent yellow lines inside the foot-ring after 1780; cobalt blue usually well controlled, except in very early pieces, and of a colour typified by Colour Plate 1—in later pieces varying up to the violet-toned blue of the Davis/Flight period, the glaze of this latter period showing a very bubbled and speckled appearance, especially under the base, and often very blued, particularly on printed ware; rims of bowls frequently found to be chamfered away on the outside.

If sufficient of these facts add up on the credit side and there are no adverse features, the *final* thing to consider is the mark—if the piece has one. This may now be used to see if it confirms the ascription already arrived at.

Plate 1 gives a sample of the marks found on the site in their actual photo-graphed form. Some of them are only found on Worcester pieces—the forms of the 'W' and the disguised numeral marks. Any pieces of genuine eighteenth century porcelain found with these marks can be regarded positively as Worcester. It is likely that the greater number of pieces bearing painters' marks are Worcester; and other marks which can be regarded as certain Worcester ones, although not found on the site, are the painted or embossed versions of the initials 'WPC' (for Worcester Porcelain Company) and the script-written word 'Flight', which is sometimes found associated with a small crescent.

As previously explained, a painted open crescent is found on painted ware and a printed lined crescent is found on pieces printed from the original copper. On repair or retouching of the copper, the various additions—first of hatchings, then of letters and man-in-the-moon faces—are made to the printed crescent. Onglaze prints do not generally have a mark. Willow-pattern type prints of the Davis/Flight period can have a printed open or hatched crescent or a disguised numeral mark.

A number of Oriental-type marks are used, some patterns having their own particular mark. The most common mark on special pieces—particularly those having scale blue decoration—is a painted blue fretted square, which can take a number of differing forms and is sometimes found associated with a small crescent.

Patterns or shapes copying other European factories often have a mark suggestive of the particular factory: for instance, the anchor of Chelsea, the crossed 'L's of Sèvres, and the swords of Meissen—although in the case of the last mark Worcester usually added a curious additional number, generally a '9' or '91' in the base of the swords.

Here a general warning about marks must be given, especially the square marks. If a fake is going to be made in an attempt to deceive, it is obvious that a mark is going to be put on it. Many thousands of fakes exist—not all of them made by the famous (or infamous) Samson firm of Paris—and some of them are now of an age when they have acquired a degree of authenticity. Plate 81 shows a genuine Worcester blue scale mug with fabulous birds together with a Continental hard paste porcelain fake next to it. Notice particularly the artificial, careful look of the fake, and the rather mechanically even look of the scales—a feature not generally seen on the genuine pieces. Most of the fakes are, of course, in hard paste porcelain and it is therefore important to be able to recognise this material.

Some ware, although copies of genuine Worcester, cannot be thought of in terms of fakes. Booths of Tunstall frequently copy Worcester shapes and patterns—in particular, plates and baskets decorated with blue and white prints such as 'blue sprays'—but these are always in earthenware and usually have the factory mark of a crescent and a 'B' conjoined. Grainger's factory in Worcester made large numbers of copies of scale blue pieces in the late nineteenth century; but these, as also the present-day versions of old patterns made by the Worcester Royal Porcelain Company, are in bone china (a very translucent material) and always bear the Company trade mark.

Some eighteenth century blue and white ware is found in a 'clobbered' state: that is, onglaze colours—usually reds and greens—and gilding have been added to a subject which is strictly complete as blue and white, in an attempt to make it a richer, more expensive piece. Clobbering usually ruins the piece artistically. It could have been done in the eighteenth century by outside decorators, but it could as well have been done at any time later. We carried out some clobbering on a teapot cover that had been buried in the ground for two hundred years and, after firing it, produced a classic eighteenth century clobbered look without showing any signs of spitting out of the glaze and other damage that would be thought a likely result of refiring an old piece.*

The most difficult faking to spot is where a genuine old Worcester piece which originally had a very simple decoration—such as the gilded 'Queen's' pattern—has the decoration removed and a more splendid onglaze painting put in its place. Here, of course, one has a genuine Worcester body. So it is necessary to look very closely at all pieces decorated in onglaze colours alone to see whether there are faint remains of an original pattern.

Summing up: the only sure way of developing the ability to recognise early Worcester is by constant handling of genuine pieces and viewing of major collections.

---

* Although the generally accepted view is that this clobbering was done 'off the factory' it has seemed to me not unlikely that a great quantity of the better quality of this work was done *in* the factory. The blue and white patterns commonly found clobbered, such as 'root', 'tambourine' and other early ones, would rapidly lose popularity after 1780 and the Company could well have been left with early types of blue patterns on their hands at a time when the favoured colour had turned to the stronger violet toned blue. In an attempt to sell off this ware it would be quite a natural thing for the Company to colour the pieces and make them saleable.

Bibliography

It is now a fact that some considerable portions of a number of earlier books about Worcester are misleading and inaccurate. Even though this is the case, most of the following books contain much that is still pertinent and of great interest; and some are now by way of being classics.

The two oldest books dealing with the subject of Worcester porcelain are important sources of early information: Valentine Green's *Survey of the City of Worcester*, J. Butler, 1764, and R. W. Binn's *A Century of Potting in the City of Worcester*, Quaritch, 1865. The latter was the first serious attempt to deal with the early history and its products, and although Binns had to make a number of intelligent guesses—for instance, at first he did not have the original Articles—it is quite amazing how accurate he was. Living so much closer to the actual events, he was able to obtain a considerable amount of information that would otherwise have been lost; and his narrative, written by one of the few practical potters to tackle such a subject, is fascinating to read.

In general, the other books of the nineteenth century—such as Jewitt's *Ceramic Art of Great Britain*, J. S. Virtue & Co. Ltd., and the early editions of Chaffer's *Marks & Monograms*, Reeves & Turner—are unreliable, as so much of their information has been proved incorrect.

Of the productions of this century the most useful books are *Worcester Porcelain* by R. L. Hobson, Quaritch, 1910, for its very fine photographs; and the same author's *Catalogue of the Frank Lloyd Collection of Worcester Porcelain of the Wall Period*, British Museum, 1925; W. J. Pountney's *Old Bristol Potteries*, J. W. Arrowsmith Ltd., 1920, for its early researches into Bristol delft and porcelain; two catalogues by Bernard Rackham of the *Herbert Allen Collection*, Victoria & Albert Museum, 1923, and the *Schreiber Collection*, Victoria & Albert Museum, 1928; an important technical book *Analysed Specimens of English Porcelain*, Victoria & Albert Museum, 1922, by Eccles & Rackham; two important books about the prints of Robert Hancock by Cyril Cook, *The Life and Work of Robert Hancock*, Chapman & Hall Ltd, 1955, and a supplementary volume in which all known Hancock engravings are illustrated and discussed; and a treatise by W. H. Tapp on *Jefferyes Hamett O'Neale*, University of London Press, 1938.

Undoubtedly the most important publication on the coloured ware is H. Rissik Marshall's *Coloured Worcester Porcelain of the First Period*, Ceramic Book Company, 1954, which, as well as showing his own magnificent collection, presents the incredible coloured Worcester ware assembled for the bi-centenary exhibition of 1951. The main single-piece illustrations are of superb quality, although the circumstances of the photographing of the main bulk of the pieces massed on shelves makes it difficult to see much detail. Nevertheless, it remains a unique book and the circumstances of being able to gather all these pieces together between two covers may never happen again.

The most important book dealing with blue and white ware is Dr. Bernard Watney's *English Blue and White Porcelain of the Eighteenth Century*, Faber & Faber, 1963. This book, written by one of the greatest experts on the earliest ware of the English porcelain factories, is a very important one—although some of the references to the later ware of Worcester and Caughley now have to be revised and the photographs of these groups likewise.

The key book relating to our newly-discovered knowledge of the relationship between Caughley and Worcester is now Geoffrey Godden's *Caughley & Worcester Porcelain, 1775–1800*, Herbert Jenkins Ltd., 1969, which deals exhaustively with the subject in a most scholarly way and must obviously be regarded as the standard work.

Other relatively recent books dealing with Worcester and Caughley, which in the light of the new discoveries need considerable revision, are F. A. Barrett's *Caughley & Coalport Porcelain*, F. Lewis Publishers Ltd, 1951 (in which a number of pieces illustrated as Caughley are in fact Worcester); the same author's *Worcester Porcelain & Lund's Bristol*, Faber & Faber, 1966; Stanley Fisher's *English Blue and White Porcelain of the 18th Century*, Batsford, 1947, and F. Severne Mackenna's *Worcester Porcelain*, 1950.

Much valuable research is to be found in the pages of the English Ceramic Circle Transactions and those of the earlier English Porcelain Circle, particularly the work done on the invention of printing on porcelain.

Readers may like to know where the most important public collections of Worcester porcelain may be found in England. Both the British Museum and the Victoria & Albert Museum in London contain very good selections, but the two finest collections are in the provinces.

The H. Rissik Marshall Collection, in the Ashmolean Museum at Oxford, contains a magnificent assembly of splendid coloured ware, including many fine examples of the work of O'Neale. The Dyson Perrins Museum at Worcester— housed in a fine, restored Victorian school—is without doubt the most comprehensive collection of Worcester of all periods in the world, and all the photographs in this book (with a very few exceptions in the cases where credits are given) are of pieces from this collection. It is hoped to be able to show a quantity of the newly excavated material at the Dyson Perrins Museum, by kind permission of the Corporation of the City of Worcester.

Index